French Country Wines

French Country
Wines

Steven Spurrier

Foreword by Hugh Johnson

Willow Books

Collins
8 Grafton Street, London W1

1984

In memory of Digby,
a French country dog

Willow Books
William Collins plc
London . Glasgow . Sydney . Auckland
Toronto . Johannesburg

Spurrier, Steven.
French country wines.
1. Wine and wine making—France
I. Title
641.2′2′0944   TP553

ISBN 0–00–218048–0

Designed and produced by
Robert Adkinson Limited, London

Editorial Director Clare Howell

Editor Hilary Dickinson

Design Rose & Lamb Design Partnership

Cartography Anne Lamb

Phototypeset in Baskerville by
Ashwell Print Services Ltd, Ashwellthorpe, Norwich

Illustrations originated by
East Anglian Engraving Co Ltd, Norwich

Printed and bound in Belgium by
Brepols, Turnhout

Contents

Foreword by Hugh Johnson 6

Introduction by Steven Spurrier 7

French Wine in the 1980s 8

The Appellation Contrôlée System 12

Vins de Pays 14

How to Use the Book 18

Regional Gazetteer

Jura, Savoie, Alsace 20

Burgundy 34

The Rhône Valley 54

Provence, the Midi, Corsica 70

Bordeaux and the South-West 102

The Loire Valley 132

Grape Varieties 158

How and Where to Buy Country Wines 162

Wine and Food 164
Temperature of Serving
Order of Serving

Vintage Chart 166
Bottle Sizes and Shapes

Glossary 168

Comités Interprofessionnels Vins et Spiritueux 170

Bibliography 171

Index 172

Acknowledgements 176

Note: Measurement conversion

Measurements of volume and area have been expressed in
hectolitres (hl) and hectares (ha):
1 hectolitre = 26.4 U.S. gallons
1 hectare = 2.471 acres

Foreword

There is an ill-kept secret about Steven Spurrier which I will unsportingly reveal: he cannot make up his mind. Ask him where he lives and he will hedge. Is it London or Paris? No answer. Neither would be accurate. He has homes, offices and shops in both cities, yet he is always somewhere else. Where? In a cellar, a vineyard, a tasting-room . . . wherever word has reached him that there is good wine to be found.

Word reached me, in the early 1970s, that Paris had suffered the shock and humiliation of finding that its wine merchant was an Englishman. Paris may have been vague about his name, but they knew his address – a mews off the rue Royale, a stone's-throw from the Madeleine. *L'anglais* (there were various spurious versions of his name) was acknowledged to be a new phenomenon: an adopted Parisian who did not just take the well-worn hierarchy of *appellations* on trust, but who bustled about France (even beyond France, said some) tasting everything, quizzing growers, bargaining with them, and returning to Paris laden with unheard-of treasures.

He also ran a remarkable little wine school, l'Académie du Vin, with an American partner, Patricia Gallagher, in the intimacy of a bar he had salvaged from some old café. Here English and American visitors to Paris flocked, to a home from home where they could learn more than almost any native could have taught them.

This is the background to Steven Spurrier's extensive knowledge of the by-ways of wine-growing France. But the scene he has mastered so thoroughly has not been a static one. Far from it: over the last ten years the backwaters of French wine have been bootstrapping themselves busily into official and unofficial notice. Vastly improved technology has been stimulated by foreign competition to raise standards at a rate nobody believed possible. Who was it who orchestrated the foreign competition, bringing France's best tasters face to face with California's best wines? It was Steven Spurrier. And I bet it has postponed his Légion d'Honneur by a good few years.

Hugh Johnson

Introduction

During the last few years the phrase 'French country wines' has become a regular feature of wine advertising, at first by the French Government and now by importers and retailers. The phrase has a nice ring to it, bringing to mind – along with country bread and country cooking – something not too sophisticated, but satisfying and genuine, good value for money. This they certainly are, and there are as many country wines in France as there are *plats* in country restaurants. This book is rather like a book of recipes, a list of these wines with brief descriptions, and an attempt to answer the question 'That wine looks interesting, I wonder where it comes from and what it tastes like'.

As regards the definition of a 'country wine', I have taken it to be a wine which is drunk by locals and tourists in the place where it is made, which has certain defined regional characteristics and is not too sophisticated or expensive. A country wine is not always cheap, but at a range of prices and income levels, it should be considered somebody's everyday wine. In this way, Saint-Emilion is a country wine, but the Grands Crus Classés Saint-Emilions are not. Burgundy is, Chambertin is not. The wine from Condrieu is mostly drunk on the spot, but it is too rare and expensive. Champagne is also drunk by the locals and tourists, in massive quantities, but the image which the Champagne producers have given to their wine together with its price exclude it from this book. Also excluded are wines with no regional characteristics. The branded wines that now make up a large proportion of French wines sold abroad are wines from different parts of the country blended to match a taste and a price. In America these are known as 'zip-code' wines, since the only regional origin on the label is the address of the bottler, itself generally more prestigious than the wine inside the bottle. Thus Mouton Cadet could be considered a country wine, since it is a Bordeaux, while Moreau Blanc could not.

The wines are set out region by region, for easy geographical identification. A shopper in a supermarket, or someone confronted with a wine list or a special offer, will be able to find the wines in the index. The book is intended to fulfil two functions: as a useful source of reference, and as an interesting fund of information to be dipped into to show the number of marvellous, and different, wines made in France. I hope that the reader will feel at least some of the pleasure of discovery in using it as I felt in writing it.

Steven Spurrier

French Wine in the 1980s

France is the second-largest wine producer in Europe, with a total of almost 1 million hectares under vines. Large as this total may seem, it is 10% less than in 1979, 20% less than in 1970 and under half the acreage planted in 1962. The basic reason for this is that consumption at home has been falling at a rate for which expanding exports cannot compensate, allied to the general move away from rural areas to the towns by the younger generation. The decrease in land under vines has mainly occurred in regions producing poor-quality wine for mass consumption, and although there are one or two small *appellations* for fine wine which are now in danger of extinction, where replanting does happen, it is to maintain or increase quality. Wine production is now the third most important agricultural element in France after grazing and cereals, representing 20.5% of all agricultural products and 9.2% of the Gross National Product. With the general decrease in land under vines, only the *départements* in the Languedoc-Roussillon are totally dependent on wine production. The total acreage of land under vines between 1962 and 1981 is shown in Table 1a; Table 1b gives the break-down into individual categories of wine in 1981.

Table 1a. Surface under vines 1962–1981

	Hectares
1962	2,300,000
1970	1,195,000
1979	1,087,000
1981	998,715

Table 1b. Surface under vines 1981: categories of wine

	Hectares
Vin de table/Vin de pays	437,421
Eau-de-vie	159,375
VDQS	94,543
AOC	307,376
Total	998,715

While the acreage under vines has fallen, production has remained remarkably stable in the last ten years. The size of the crop in proportion to the number of vines planted is determined by the weather: the absence of spring frosts, the need for dry sunny weather at the flowering in June and not too wet ripening conditions to prevent rot, all these used to be necessary to produce a satisfactory crop. Today, better fertilization, protective measures against frost and improved treatments against disease and rot produce a higher average yield per hectare. The final crop is very variable, however, as can be seen from Table 2. These figures also show the increasing percentage of AOC wines, indicating that while quantity is perhaps falling, quality is rising. In 1981 the total value of wine produced in France was 18,108 million francs, of which AOC and VDQS represented 10,292 million and *vins courants* (everyday wines) 7,816 million francs. The break-down of wine produced per region in 1982 is shown in Table 3.

Table 2. Wine production 1970–1982

(million hectolitres)

	Total	AOC	Other wines
1970	74.70	11.40	63.00
1978	58.17	12.53	46.64
1979	83.54	16.77	66.77
1980	69.20	12.91	56.29
1981	57.01	12.00	45.01
1982	79.20	19.80	59.40

Table 3. Wine production in 1982

Region	Total %
Alsace	1.98
Aquitaine	9.93
Burgundy	2.18
Champagne	3.00
Corsica	1.83
Languedoc – Roussillon	37.05
Midi – Pyrénées	6.32
Poitou – Charentes	16.87
Provence – Côte d'Azur	8.73
Rhône – Alpes	4.96
Loire Valley – Centre	6.51
Other regions	0.64
(*Source:* Onivit – INAO)	

While total production remains consistent with, and in plentiful years in excess of, total demand, consumption at home has been falling regularly. The French now drink (only) 80 litres of wine per head per year as opposed to 120 litres in 1969. However, while they are drinking less, it is of better quality (Table 4).

Table 4. Wine consumption in France

(million hectolitres)

	Total	AOC	Other wines
1970	45.98	5.49	40.49
1978	45.75	7.23	38.52
1979	44.21	7.39	36.82
1980	43.66	8.03	35.53
1981	43.20	8.70	34.50

On the export front the volume of wine is increasing in actual terms, in value terms and as a percentage of the production (Table 5). In 1979, 11% of the crop was exported, in 1980, 12.7%. In 1980, 21% of all AOC wines was exported (47% of the total value of exports). Although 60% of exports goes to the EEC, the United States are the single largest purchaser. Britain is second, with an astounding increase of 60% in imports of vins de pays in 1981–2.

Table 5. Wine exports 1970–1980

	Volume (million hectolitres)	Value (million francs)
1970	3.81	2,515
1977	7.92	4,791
1978	7.20	5,955
1979	8.20	6,878
1980	8.87	7,323

As regards production and sales, France has essentially an ancient pattern of land-holding, where the vineyards have become so parcellated through inheritance that very many families own very small amounts of land. This is unprofitable, and the trend is for greater consolidation. In 1982 there were 429,000 people making wine in France, of whom 236,000 regularly sell commercially, the remaining 193,000 keeping the wine for home consumption (5% of the total annual quantity of wine made). Only 30,000 of these *exploitants* own more than 10 hectares of vines, but they own more than 50% of the land under vines. The very large number with less than 2 hectares represents less than 10% of the total acreage. That there will be further changes is evident from the fact that 20.8% of the growers are aged 65 and over, while only 3.3% are under 30. Of all *exploitants*, 27% have another job. The rise in importance and quality of the vins de pays seems to have arrested the wholesale tearing-up of unprofitable vineyards, and in order to achieve increased benefit, vineyard holdings will have to be made more efficient. The larger the domaine, the more the production of wine predominates, although most still maintain a second activity, such as farming.

Ownership by *négociants* is only important in the AOC vineyards and is about 10% over all. In Alsace, *négociants* own only 3% of the vineyards, in Champagne 12% and in Burgundy and Bordeaux around 5%. It is very small in the South, despite the presence of the Salins du Midi (Listel), Nicolas and Chantovent. Foreign interest is negligible and is concentrated among the very finest *crus. Négociants*, however, commercialize 50% of French wines.

The Coopérative movement owns between 480,000 and 500,000 hectares. A Cave Coopérative is a group of wine-growers who either cannot, by virtue of the size of their holding, or do not wish to, make their own wine or commercialize it. The Coopérative buys all the heavy machinery for use in the vines, purchases the grapes from the grower, makes the wine and is responsible for selling it, returning to the grower the money for his grapes and/or a quantity of bottles. The Caves Coopératives produce 45.8% of French wine, 60% of the *vin de table*, 42.8% of the AOC and VDQS wines. They are of great importance in the Languedoc-Roussillon: 67% of *vin de table*, 62% of the quality wines. Membership rose from 120,000 in 1939 to 290,000 in 1969 and has now fallen to 260,000.

What for the future? There is a strong resurgence of interest in wine in France at all levels. The blanket of *gros rouge* has been lifted, and everyone has realized that quality pays. The willingness of French wine-drinkers to experiment with different wines has developed only in the last ten years. Consumers, French and foreign alike, are looking for wines with individual character and regional definition. The AOCs and VDQSs have this, and the vins de pays are acquiring it. One of the aims of this book is to help the consumer find his way through the maze of French wines since an informed wine-drinker buys well, and supporting the good French wine-makers will benefit lovers of wine both in France and abroad.

The Appellation Contrôlée System

The French system of *appellation contrôlée*, which has been the inspiration of controlling the place names of wines in Europe, and of recent attempts to do the same in California, is primarily geographical in nature: it tells the wine-drinker where the wine comes from, be it a region (Bourgogne), a commune (Gevrey-Chambertin) or a *grand cru* (Chambertin). The aim of the Institut National des Appellations d'Origine (INAO) is that a wine carrying a certain name should correspond to a certain style, based on where the vines are planted. Further controls are on the types of grape varieties that may be planted and in what proportion, the minimum degree of natural sugar in the grape juice before fermentation and sometimes a maximum degree after fermentation, the yield per hectare, the method of pruning and looking after the vines, and in some cases the method and length of ageing. What cannot be controlled is the man who makes the wine, so it has to be submitted to official tastings to see that it conforms to its *appellation*.

There are three main types of *vin d'appellation*:
1. Vin d'Appellation d'Origine Contrôlée (AOC)
2. Vin Délimité de Qualité Supérieure (VDQS)
3. Vin de Pays

There is a fourth type, Vin de Table, blended wine, usually sold under a brand name with no regional origin.

It has been said that the grape variety gives the wine its personality, while the soil gives it its soul. The idea of *appellation* is inseparable from the concept of *terroir*, the combination of soil and climate that gives each wine a certain style. Some *terroirs* are less dominant than others, and the personality of the grape will come through more. In general, the more typical a wine is in each *appellation*, the more pronounced the *terroir*. This is especially true of country wines.

The controls on the minimum alcohol content and the yield are interlocked. In both cases the minimum is low, and is generally exceeded. With the exception of the southern vineyards and the vins de pays, the degree of alcohol may be increased by chaptalization, the adding to the must of sugar that merges with the natural grape sugar to be transformed into alcohol. The yield is often exceeded as a result either of good harvests or of efficiency in fighting vineyard diseases. Yet, even with improved methods of viticulture and vinification, it is rare that a very large yield makes a wine of high quality, and it remains an axiom of quality that a reasonable yield will provide for a reasonable degree of natural alcohol and make a better-balanced wine.

How to Read a Label

AOC: Bourgogne Aligoté

mention that the wine is bottled on grower's premises

obligatory contents

name of wine

AOC

name and address of grower

Note: The vintage will be on the collarette label

VDQS: Cheverny

VDQS guarantee label, with its number

name of wine

grape variety (not obligatory)

volume of wine now 75 cl

wine bottled on the property

name and address and telephone number of grower

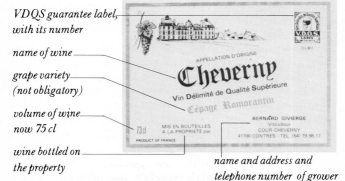

Note: The vintage will be on the collarette label

Vin de Pays: Coteaux de la Cité de Carcassonne

vintage

name of vineyard

Vin de Pays de Zone

bottled on the property

mention that it is French wine (not obligatory)

contents

name and address of owner

Vins de Pays

While all aspects of French viticulture are controlled by decrees from the Minister of Agriculture, the vins de pays present such an ever-changing scene that one might think that the *vignerons* were in charge rather than the Government. In a country where the vast majority of *vins d'appellation* have a style and character that have evolved for several generations and are now recognizable and classified, the classification of vins de pays is a relatively new part of French wine production. Vins de pays came into being officially in 1968, when a decree was passed authorizing certain *vins de table* to indicate the regional origin of the wine. This was designed to inform the consumer and to give him certain guarantees of origin. In 1973, a further decree fixed precisely the conditions of production to which a vin de pays must adhere in order to have the right to the *appellation*: the region, grape varieties, yield, alcohol content, even the level of SO_2 and volatile acidity. Finally, in 1979, these conditions were refined and particular rules were established for individual vins de pays in an effort to increase the quality. The aim throughout has been the same as for the more important AOCs and VDQSs, namely that the consumer must be offered a wine with a guarantee of origin which, being easily identifiable, should provide him with an assurance as to the quality of the final product.

The decree of 1973 did away with the Vins d'Appellation d'Origine Simple (AOS), leaving the vins de pays as the only category of personalized *vins de table*. In all, there are three basic types of vin de pays, corresponding to different geographical interpretations:

1. Vins de Pays Régionaux These may come from several *départements* as long as they correspond to an accepted style of wine, for example Vin de Pays d'Oc, for the whole of the Languedoc-Roussillon; Vin de Pays du Jardin de la

France, for wines from the Loire Valley.

2. *Vins de Pays Départementaux* These must carry the name of the *département* where they are produced, for example Vin de Pays du Gard, Vin de Pays de l'Ardèche.

3. *Vins de Pays de Zone* These wines may state the name of the individual commune where they are produced, for example Vin de Pays du Val d'Orbieu (Aude), Vin de Pays des Coteaux du Salavès (Gard).

All vins de pays fit into one or another of these categories, and it is plain that category (3) can be sold as categories (2) and (1), and category (2) as (1) if it is desirable to do so.

The rules governing the production of *vins de table* follow the same pattern as for the other *appellations*. First, they must have geographical identity, from a specified region; second, they may only be made from 'recommended' grape varieties, of which the list is fixed by decree (these are in most cases the grape varieties used for the more important wines of the region, with the addition of *cépages nobles* if the soil and climate are suitable); third, the yield per hectare must not exceed 80 hl for the Vins de Pays de Zone, 90 hl for the Vins de Pays Départementaux; fourth, the minimum alcohol content must be 9° for the north of France and the Alpes-du-Nord, 9.5° for the South-West, the Rhône Valley and the Alpes-du-Sud, and 10° for the Languedoc-Roussillon, Provence and Corsica; fifth, the level of SO_2 and volatile acidity is strictly controlled and the wine must pass an official tasting before being allowed to be sold as vin de pays.

The volume of vins de pays produced is immense, averaging 5.5 million hectolitres a year (630 million bottles), about 14% of the total French production. Vins de pays are produced in 45 *départements*, but are concentrated in the Languedoc-Roussillon region, which represents 75% of the production, with the *département* of the Pyrénées-Orientales alone accounting for 20%. Provence–Côte d'Azur accounts for a further 12% and the

Loire Valley for 6%. There are 92 separate Vins de Pays de Zone, to which must be added the 45 Vins de Pays Départementaux and the three Vins de Pays Régionaux, making a total of 150 possible types of vins de pays. It should also be remembered that over 10% of the wines presented for classification as vins de pays are rejected by the Tasting Commission.

It is not surprising that a large part of this volume is produced by the Caves Coopératives. On a national level, the 1,200 Caves Coopératives in France produce a fraction over half the total of all table wine. For the vins de pays, this rises to 64%, against 36% from privately owned Caves. Many of the Vins de Pays de Zone are produced almost entirely by one Cave Coopérative. Furthermore, with the vast quantity of wine involved, the Coopératives are now marketing their wine as well as producing it.

While for the everyday drinker of French wine, vins de pays would seem to offer an unlimited range of genuine country wines, the French Government is not totally satis-fied with their progress. The reason lies in the multiplicity of labels and the, as yet, lack of a defined *image de marque*. On the production side, many *vignerons* consider the vin de pays label merely as a stepping-stone to the higher categories of VDQS or even AOC, while the Government wishes to promote vin de pays as an *appellation* in its own right. From the consumer's point of view, the increasing number of wines available causes confusion and disorien-tation. As a middleman, the *négociant* is often hesitant to purchase a wine with a little-known name, possibly from a single Cave Coopérative, where he may not be assured of a supply every year, while on the other hand he may find the regional vins de pays, the Vin de Pays d'Oc, for example, from a basket of 7 *départements*, too vague for the concept of regional origin to play a part. As a result, big *négociants* may prefer to build up a *vin de marque* under their own name. At the same time, the *vignerons* are unwilling to see their wine disappearing into an anonymous 'zip-code' product, or even bottled under a *négociant*'s label, and are beginning to bottle their own wine, marketing it direct.

In the midst of this confusion, there are two very encouraging elements. The first is the commitment by the Ministry of Agriculture and the positive reaction from the producers to maintain quality. Wine consumption in France is falling, with the noticeable drop being in the consumption of *vin ordinaire*. While this may please the Anti-Alcohol League, it does not please the wine-growers, who have more votes. With higher-quality vin de pays, the French are drinking less, but better, wine, while export markets are being re-convinced that French wines are good value for money. The second element is the introduction of *cépages nobles* into the production of vins de pays. The role played by the grape variety in the taste and style of a wine is as great as that played by the soil and climate. The major *appellations* in France have evolved and refined their varietal base over centuries, and the principles of what varieties should be planted where underlie the whole system of Appellation Contrôlée. For years it had been assumed that wines from the Midi could only be made from *cépages méridionaux*, and only in the last decade have experiments proved that the grapes that make France's finest wines may produce excellent, individual wines outside their region of origin. Thus, little by little, we are seeing Cabernet Sauvignon, Merlot, Chardonnay and Sauvignon appearing on the labels of vins de pays. This development is in its infancy, but it is gathering strong support from Caves Coopératives as well as from innovative growers. The wines are generally successful, retaining their varietal characteristics along with the intrinsic style of the region. There are two main advantages for French viticulture, and for the consumer: the name of the grape gives a varietal image to the wine, easier to recognize than a geographical one; and the price is that of a vin de pays.

How to Use the Book

The book is divided into the six major wine-producing regions of France: the Eastern vineyards of Jura, Savoie and Alsace; Burgundy, including Chablis and Beaujolais; the Rhône Valley; Provence, the Midi, Languedoc, Roussillon, Corsica; Bordeaux and the South-West; the Loire Valley. These major regions are divided further into sub-regions, from either the point of view of geography or style, or both, with a short introduction to each. The individual wines are listed, each with a short description, in the following order: AOC, VDQS, Vins de Pays, arranged alphabetically.

The listing of alcohol content, yield and grape varieties for each wine may seem repetitive, but this is deliberate as the book is intended as a source of reference for people who may wish to look up just one wine. However, for those seeking more general information, it can be read section by section. The descriptions of what the wines taste like and with what food they may be drunk are personal, but should correspond to general opinion.

There is no rating of quality for the wines, but there is one of price, which is sometimes the same thing. The most logical pricing system is based on the price per bottle charged by the producer for his wine to *négociants*, without French value added tax. Apart from some sudden rise in popularity for a particular region or an individual wine, prices change according to supply and demand and inflation. The relation between the less expensive and more expensive wines remains fairly constant. The price code used in the book is set out below, translated into retail prices including local taxes in francs, pounds and dollars.

	FF per bottle export	FF retail	£ retail	$ retail
A	up to 7.50	up to 14.00	up to 2.50	up to 3.75
B	7.50–10.00	15.00–20.00	2.50–3.00	3.75–4.50
C	10.00–15.00	20.00–30.00	3.00–3.75	4.50–5.50
D	15.00–20.00	30.00–40.00	3.75–4.75	5.50–7.00
E	20.00–30.00	40.00–60.00	4.75–6.50	7.00–10.00
F	30.00 and over	60.00 and over	6.50 and over	10.00 and over

VIGNOBLES DE FRANCE

CHAMPAGNE
ALSACE
VAL-DE-LOIRE
BOURGOGNE
COGNAC
BEAUJOLAIS
SAVOIE
BORDEAUX
BERGERAC
CAHORS
COTES-DU-RHONE
ARMAGNAC
LANGUEDOC
COTES-DE-PROVENCE
ROUSSILLON
CORSE

SOPEXA - COMITÉ NATIONAL DES VINS DE FRANCE
43, rue de Naples 75008 PARIS

Jura, Savoie, Alsace

The wines of the Jura all come from the *département* of the
same name, from what were once the vineyards of the
Franche-Comté. The vines are planted on favourably
exposed slopes of the Jura hills, along a line about 80 kilometres long and 6 kilometres wide parallel to the vineyards
of the Côte d'Or. What the area lacks in volume of production, it makes up for in the variety of its wines: they are
red, white, rosé, *gris* and sparkling, not forgetting the
remarkable *vin jaune* and *vin de paille*. These last two wines
are some of the rarest in France and by virtue of their price
should not be considered as country wines. However, the
opportunity to purchase them outside the Jura is so limited
that they fit into the category of local wines drunk on the
spot. The Jura has its own grape varieties, the red Poulsard
and Trousseau and the white Savagnin, and the Pinot Noir
and Chardonnay from nearby Burgundy are also planted.
The flavour and character of wines from the Jura are very
marked, especially that of the white wines. They are old-
fashioned wines, sometimes difficult to balance with food,
but most individual and interesting.

The Savoie vineyards, extending over the *départements* of
the Savoie, Haute-Savoie and a few communes of the Ain
and the Isère, are known principally for their white wine.
As with the wines of Alsace, they benefit (or suffer, as the
case may be) from a global image of *vins de Savoie*, while the

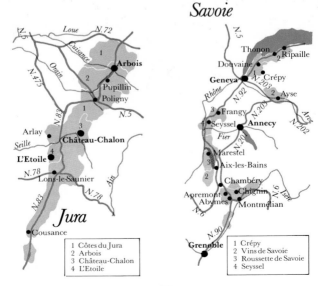

1	Côtes du Jura
2	Arbois
3	Château-Chalon
4	L'Etoile

1	Crépy
2	Vins de Savoie
3	Roussette de Savoie
4	Seyssel

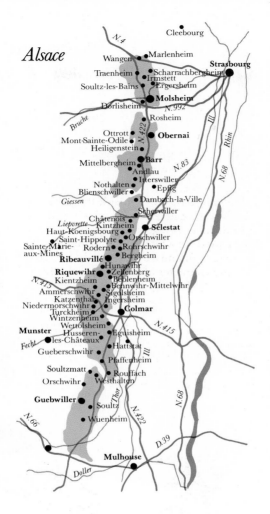

Alsace

Cleebourg

Marlenheim
Wangen
Traenheim • Scharrachbergheim
Irmstett
Soultz-les-Bains • Ergersheim
Strasbourg
N.4

Dorlisheim • **Molsheim**
N.992
Bruche
Rosheim

Ottrott
Mont-Sainte-Odile • **Obernai**
Heiligenstein
N.422

Mittelbergheim • **Barr**
Andlau
Itterswiller
Nothalten • Epfig
Blienschwiller
Giessen
Dambach-la-Ville
Scherwiller
N.83
N.68

Châtenois
Liepvrette • Kintzheim
Haut-Koenigsbourg • **Sélestat**
Saint-Hippolyte • Orschwiller
Rodern • Rohrschwihr
Sainte-Marie-
aux-Mines
Bergheim
Ribeauvillé
Hunawihr
Riquewihr • Zellenberg
Kientzheim • Beblenheim
Ammerschwihr • Bennwihr-Mittelwihr
Katzenthal • Sigolsheim
Niedermorschwihr • Ingersheim
Turckheim
Wintzenheim • **Colmar**
Wettolsheim
Munster • Husseren-Eguisheim
Fecht les-Châteaux
Hattstatt
Gueberschwihr
Pfaffenheim
Soultzmatt
Orschwihr • Rouffach
Westhalten
Guebwiller
Soultz
N.66 • Wuenheim
N.422
Thor
Ill
Rhin
N.68
N.415

D.39

Mulhouse
Doller

individual wines receive less attention. In fact, while the basic style of these wines is light, pale in colour, with a smoky-fruity bouquet and crisp dry finish, there are also some richer white wines made, some delicious reds and rosés and a great deal of sparkling wine. The difference between these wines is evident from the label, which will state either the village or commune the wine comes from, or the grape variety it is made with.

In Alsace, the wine country covers a stretch of hill-side vineyards roughly 100 kilometres long and 1 to 5 kilometres wide between the Vosges Mountains and the Rhine Valley in the Haut-Rhin and Bas-Rhin *départements* in the north-east of France. With the exception of a pocket of vines in the north at Cleebourg, just by the German border, the vines run without a break from Marlenheim, on the same level as Strasbourg, to Thann, on a level with Mulhouse. The climate is remarkably sunny and dry, thanks to the shelter from the wind and rain from the north-west afforded by the Vosges Mountains, and Colmar, the centre of the Alsatian wine industry, has the second lowest rainfall in France after Perpignan. The slopes have an excellent exposition for vines, facing south-south-east, at a level of 200–450 metres, ensuring maximum sun throughout the ripening period, and even allowing the late-harvesting of fully botrytised grapes in good years. Alsace has only one *appellation*, Alsace, but many permitted grape varieties. It is these, allied to the diversity of the soil (chalky-clay, sandy-gravel, sandstone and silt) and distinctive micro-climates, that give the wines of Alsace their wide range of styles.

Jura

A wide variety of wines are produced from the vineyards in the Jura *département*, red, white, rosé, *gris* and sparkling wines, as well as the specialities *vin jaune* and *vin de paille*. All the wines from the Jura are distinctive and full of character.

Arbois AOC

Red, dry white, *gris* and rosé wines from vineyards planted around the town of Arbois in the centre of the Jura wine country. The red wines may be made from Trousseau, Poulsard or Pinot Noir grapes, either alone or blended. The Trousseau makes a deep-coloured, full-bodied *vin-de-garde*, the Poulsard a much lighter wine with great finesse, and is often reserved for rosés, while the Pinot Noir wines much resemble the lighter Côte de Beaune. Rosé d'Arbois is well known for its faded, pale red 'onion-skin' colour, the appearance of a rosé with the body of a red wine. White wines are made from the Savagnin, which has the most pronounced slightly sherry-like Jura style, the Chardonnay or Pinot Blanc. Especially when made with the Savagnin, the whites are full yellow in colour, with a distinctive nutty bouquet, a rich intensity of flavour and completely dry. They are good drunk just on their own, but are at their best with fish or chicken in a cream sauce, preferably one to which the same wine has been added. Production of Arbois wines is limited to 40 hl/ha with an alcohol content of 10° for the reds and 10.5° for the whites. Total production is in the region of 2 million bottles a year, of which 40% is white. Price D–E.

Arbois Mousseux AOC

Sparkling wine made by the *méthode champenoise* with wines from the Arbois *appellation*. The genuine sparkling wine from Arbois is of high quality and should not be confused with a cheaper version called *vin fou*. Price D–E.

Arbois Pupillin AOC

Red, dry white and rosé wines from the commune of Pupillin, where the soil gives an added intensity of flavour to the wines. Very little seen. Price E.

Côtes du Jura AOC

Red, dry white, *gris* and rosé wines from vineyards in the southern part of the Jura region. Red, *gris* and rosé wines are made from the Poulsard, Trousseau or Pinot Noir, either separately or together, while the whites are from the Savagnin, Chardonnay or Pinot Blanc.

Yield is limited to 40 hl/ha, not often attained in these hilly vineyards susceptible to frost, and the minimum alcohol content is 10° for the reds, *gris* and rosés, 10.5° for the whites. The Côtes du Jura are very much in the style of the Arbois wines. Production averages around 1.5 million bottles, of which 80% is white. Price D.

Côtes du Jura Mousseux AOC

Sparkling wine made by the *méthode champenoise* with wines from the Côtes du Jura *appellation*. The Savagnin grape has too distinctive a flavour, so the grapes used are Chardonnay and Pinot Blanc. Price D–E.

L'Etoile AOC

White wines only from particularly well-situated vineyards just north of Lons-le Saunier made from the Savagnin, Chardonnay and Poulsard this last vinified as a white wine. They have more finesse than the wines from Arbois and are much sought after, especially to accompany river-fish in a cream sauce. There is also some excellent sparkling wine with its own *appellation* L'Etoile Mousseux, and some *vin jaune* and *vin de paille*. Only 180,000 bottles are produced annually. Price E.

Vin de Paille

Vin de paille is, with *vin jaune*, the other rarity produced in the Jura. It is a dessert wine made from bunches of grapes that have been left for up to 2 months on large straw mats (*lits de paille*, whence the name) while the juice dries out and the sugar concentration intensifies. The result is an astoundingly rich, amber-coloured nectar, which almost more resembles a liqueur than a wine. *Vin de paille* is sold in special half bottles which are called *pots*. It is very rare and accordingly very expensive. Price F.

Vin Jaune

This is not an *appellation*, but a type of wine made in the Arbois and Jura *appellations*. The word *jaune* comes from the colour the wine acquires through its unique ageing process. The only grape permitted is the Savagnin, and after fermentation following a very late harvest (the grapes are sometimes picked when snow is on the ground) the wine is racked into oak barrels where it remains on ullage, with no topping-up allowed, for a minimum of 6 years. The result, which defies the rules of oenology, is a wine of deep yellow colour, with a heady, nutty bouquet of great complexity and the flavour of concentrated fino sherry. Having survived this system of ageing, *vin jaune* is virtually indestructible, and may keep for over a hundred years. All *vin jaune* is sold in a special squat bottle called a *clavelin*, containing 62 centilitres. The best-known *vin jaune* is Château-Chalon, which has its own *appellation*. Price F.

Savoie

Although known mainly for its crisp white wines, Savoie produces additionally a range of richer whites, very good reds and rosés and sparkling wines.

Crépy AOC

Dry white wines, that are faintly sparkling or *perlant*, from the Haute-Savoie, to the north-west of Geneva. The wines of Crépy must be made exclusively with the Chasselas grape, known as the Fendant in nearby Switzerland. They have a low alcohol content, 9° minimum, and a high natural acidity which, combined with their hint of sparkle, makes them extremely refreshing. They are more than just a thirst-quencher, however, with a lovely pale golden colour, a hint of violets on the nose, followed by a lively flavour and stylish finish. Due to the acidity, they age well, losing their freshness but becoming more complex. Crépy is generally sold in a distinctive tall green bottle. Production is only 250,000 bottles. Price D–E.

Roussette de Savoie AOC

ROUSSETTE
APPELLATION D'ORIGINE CONTROLÉE

Dry white wines from the Savoie, Haute-Savoie and a very small part of the Isère *départements*. The grape varieties are the Altesse and Chardonnay (called charmingly Petite-Sainte-Marie in the Savoie) to a maximum of 50%, with Mondeuse Blanche for the rest. Minimum alcohol content is 10°, from a low yield of 35 hl/ha. Roussette de Savoie is very dry, with good fruit, an attractive acidity and some finesse. Good as an aperitif, with *charcuterie*, fish and poultry. Production is around 250,000 bottles. Price C–D.

Roussette de Savoie + *Cru* AOC

Dry white wines grown in the Savoie and Haute-Savoie *départements*, made exclusively from the Altesse grape. The following communes have the right to add their name to that of Roussette de Savoie, or sell under their own name: Frangy, Marestel, Monterminod and Monthoux. These wines, especially those made in the commune of Marestel, have more fruit, flavour and finesse than the Roussette de Savoie *tout court*. They are absolutely perfect drunk on the spot with fresh river-fish. Production is small and very little is exported. Price D.

Seyssel *AOC*

Dry white wines from the commune of Seyssel in the Haute-Savoie and the Ain *départements*, the *appellation* being separated by the river Rhône. The vines are planted on south-south-west-facing slopes at 200–400 metres, on a chalky limestone soil. The only grape permitted is the Roussette, with a minimum alcohol content of 10° from a maximum yield of 40 hl/ha. Seyssel, which, with Crépy, was for a long time the only AOC in the Savoie, is light and dry, with a distinctive floral bouquet of violets and irises and a beautifully balanced finish. It is delicious as an aperitif, with fish or white meats and the local cheeses. Production is small, around 180,000 bottles, and little of it leaves France. Price C–D.

Seyssel Mousseux *AOC*

White sparkling wines made in the Seyssel *appellation* from the Roussette and Chasselas grapes. The wines are wonderfully light, with none of the aggressiveness characteristic of some *vins mousseux*, and most of the 80,000 bottles made a year are drunk locally. Price D–E.

Vin de Savoie *AOC*

Red, dry white and rosé wines produced in the *départements* of the Savoie, Haute-Savoie, the Ain and the Isère. The reds and rosés, often called *clairets* in the region, must come from the Mondeuse, Gamay and Pinot Noir, and while 20% white grapes may be added at fermentation, this rarely happens. Wines from the Mondeuse are particularly good, with a deep colour and a smooth fruit flavour. The Pinot Noir and the Gamay make attractive, fruity wines, quite light in colour, that should be drunk young and served cool. The better white wines are made from the local grapes Jacquère and Altesse, which give a particularly Savoie character to the wine as well as more intensity of flavour. Other white grapes are the Chardonnay, Aligoté and the Chasselas, producing agreeable, crisp, dry wines. They are good as an aperitif, with hors d'œuvres, fish and chicken, and, of course, a cheese fondue. The reds may be treated like a light Burgundy or Beaujolais. All wines must have a minimum alcohol content of 9° from a yield of 45 hl/ha. Total production 7 million bottles, two-thirds of which is white. Price C.

Vin de Savoie + Cru *AOC*

In 1973, when *vin de Savoie* became an *appellation*, certain communes or *crus* were singled out to be allowed to add their name to the label, or even sell under the name of the commune, the *appellation* remaining *vin de Savoie*. Red, dry white and rosé wines are made, as well as some excellent sparkling wine by the *méthode champenoise*. To maintain their superiority over the plain *vin de Savoie*, these wines must have a higher minimum alcohol content at 9.5° from a much lower yield of 35 hl/ha. The villages with the right to sell wine under their own name are listed alphabetically, with the better wines in italics: *Abymes*, *Apremont*, Arbin, *Ayse*, Charpinnat, *Chautagne* (reds), *Chignin*, *Chignin-Bergeron*, Cruet, Marignan, *Montmélian* (reds), *Ripaille*, Saint-Jean-de-la-Porte, Saint-Jeorie-Prieuré, Sainte-Marie-d'Alloix. The white wines are for the most part made with the Jacquère and are very good indeed. Price C–D.

Vin de Savoie *Ayse Mousseux* AOC

Sparkling wine made from grapes grown in the commune of Ayse. The grape varieties must be indigenous: the Gringet, Altesse and up to 30% Roussette d'Ayse. Production is limited to 40 hl/ha, as opposed to 45 hl for the plain Savoie Mousseux *appellation*. The wines are very elegant and most of the production is consumed locally or in Switzerland or Lyon. Price E.

Vin de Savoie *Mousseux* AOC

White and a very little rosé wine produced from vines which are grown in the Savoie by the *méthode champenoise*. The best of these come from the *cru* Ayse, although good wines also come from Chignin, Marignan and Ripaille. Sparkling wines from the Savoie are very pale in colour, often only slightly effervescent, and always dry. There is a large *vin mousseux* industry based in the Savoie that uses wine which is brought from outside the region and, however good these products may be, they have no right to the *appellation*. Price D–E.

Bugey

The wines of the Bugey come from vineyards planted in the Ain *département*, midway between the Beaujolais and the Savoie. Until recently there was a risk that the *appellation*, a VDQS, would die out, but the production, although small, has been growing owing to local demand, especially from restaurateurs. The wines are light and attractive, the reds resembling the wines of the Beaujolais, the whites those of the Savoie, but with their own particular *terroir*.

Vin du Bugey VDQS

Red, dry white and rosé wines from vines planted in the Ain *département*, around the towns of Bellet and Nantua. The reds and rosés must come from the Gamay, Pinot Noir, Poulsard or Mondeuse grapes, with the possibility of adding 20% white grapes. They are light-coloured, fruity and should be drunk young. The white wines are slightly more interesting and individual, being made from the Savoie grapes Altesse, Jacquère and Mondeuse Blanche with some Chardonnay, Aligoté and Pinot Gris. If a Bugey wine comes entirely from a single grape variety, it will say so on the label. All wines are light in alcohol, with a minimum of 9°

from a yield of 45 hl/ha. They are delightful, light, refreshing wines which are very well suited to the local cuisine of *écrevisses* and *quenelles*. The Vins du Bugey represent an excellent example of the renaissance of country wines. About a million bottles are produced annually from the entire *appellation*, 60% white. Price B–C.

Vin du Bugey + Cru VDQS

Red, dry white and rosé wines from the *appellation* Bugey, with the right to add the name of the commune to the label, or to sell the wine under the name of the *cru* itself. Five communes have this right: Virieu-le-Grand, Montagnieu, Manicle, Machuraz and Cerdon, but only Montagnieu and Cerdon

take advantage of it. The latter is always red or rosé, the former always white. Apart from the *terroir* which distinguishes the wine, the alcohol content must be a little higher at 9.5° minimum, from a lower yield of 40 hl/ha. These wines are certainly well worth the small extra expense. Price C.

Vin du Bugey Mousseux or Pétillant VDQS

Dry white sparkling wine made either by the *méthode champenoise*, or by natural fermentation in the bottle. The latter produces less sparkle, but leaves the wine all its finesse. The wines of Cerdon have their own *appellation* as *vins mousseux*, but

the finest sparkling wines come from Montagnieu. Production unfortunately is tiny, what the French call *confidentiel*, and it is mostly consumed in the local restaurants. It is a perfect aperitif and very good with the light Bugey cuisine. Price D.

Vins de Pays

Balmes Dauphinoises

Red, dry white and rosé wines from the Isère *département*. The wines are similar to the *vins de Savoie*, but a little less distinctive. The reds and rosés must be made from the Gamay, Pinot Noir and Mondeuse, to which may be

added the Syrah, Merlot and the Gamay Teinturiers. In fact, most of the wine is made from the Gamay. The whites, more interesting and excellent *vins de comptoirs*, are from the Chardonnay and the Jacquère, with the Aligoté and Pinot Gris admitted. They are light and refreshing.

Coteaux du Grésivaudan

Red, dry white and rosé wines from the Isère and Savoie *départements*. The reds and rosés are from the Gamay and Pinot Noir, the whites from the same varietals as the Vins de Pays des Balmes Dauphinoises, which they very much resemble. Production is quite large for a vin de pays from this part of France, at 500,000 bottles.

Franche-Comté

Red, dry white and rosé wines from vines planted in the *départements* of the Jura and the Haute-Saône. Grapes allowed are the Pinot Noir and Gamay for the reds and rosés, and Chardonnay, Pinot Gris and Auxerrois (Pinot Blanc) for the whites. The white wines are much the best, with a clean fruit and refreshingly crisp finish. Production averages around 200,000 bottles. Price A.

Vin de Pays de l'Ain

Very small production of mostly white wine that otherwise would have the *appellation* Vin de Bugey.

Alsace

Alsace offers a notable diversity of styles of wine, thanks to a combination of several natural factors: the variety of the soil, the propitious climate and the large number of grape varietals.

Alsace AOC

Red, rosé, dry white and sweet white wines from the Haut-Rhin and Bas-Rhin *départements*. Total land under vines is 11,600 hectares, two-thirds in the Haut-Rhin, one-third in the Bas-Rhin, producing an average annual yield of 115 million bottles, 95% white and dry. Very little red and rosé is made, and a tiny amount of *vendange tardive* sweet white wines. All wines must have a minimum alcohol content of 8.5° before chaptalization, the lowest permitted in France, from a maximum yield of 100 hl/ha, the highest permitted for AOC wines. The white wines vary from very pale yellow to a full, greeny gold, and all share a heady, perfumed bouquet. They are more or less dry, intense and complex depending on the grape and where grown. Listed below are the grape varieties planted in Alsace and the type of wines made from them.

Chasselas

The Chasselas grape is at its best in the AOC Crépy (Savoie) and in Switzerland where it produces the Fendant and the Dorin wines. In Alsace it makes a light, agreeable wine, low in acidity, to be drunk young. Most of the wine goes into the blend known as Edelzwicker, and Chasselas is almost never seen on a wine label. Planting of Chasselas is in regression in favour of the Sylvaner and the Pinot Blanc. Price B–C.

Edelzwicker

Edelzwicker is not a grape variety, but a blend of two or more noble grape varieties. It is always white and dry, with the typical Alsace flowery aromas, refreshing and easy to drink on its own or with a meal. This wine has superseded the less good Zwicker. Many *négociants* and Caves Coopératives in Alsace bring out a straightforward 'Vin d'Alsace' under a brand name, usually a blend of Chasselas and Sylvaner, that is light and crisp. Price C.

Gewürztraminer

After the Sylvaner, Gewürztraminer is the most widely planted grape in Alsace, representing just under 20% of vines in production. The wines are heavily perfumed, with an exuberant spiciness and are mouthfillingly *gras* on the palate. The exotic fruit flavours are sometimes reminiscent of lychees. Gewürztraminer should have a certain concentration, but not be overblown and heavy, which spoils the liveliness of the fruit. In good years, this grape variety makes some of the finest *vendange tardive* wines. With their aromatic spiciness, these wines can stand up to rich or exotic food, as well as being delicious on their own. Except for the late-harvest wines, which are very expensive, Gewürztraminer should be drunk relatively young, at 2 to 4 years. The best wines are made between Sélestat and Colmar. Price D–E–F.

Klevner or Clevner

These are the Alsatian names for the Pinot Blanc and Auxerrois. The Pinot Blanc is gaining in reputation, and is now sold under its own name. The wine has more aroma and body than the Sylvaner and makes very good wine in Pfaffenheim and Westhalten. Price C–D.

Muscat

Two types of Muscat are planted in Alsace, the Muscat à Petits Grains and the Muscat d'Ottonel. The former gives a wine with more body and fruit, but it is susceptible to rot; the latter has the pronounced Muscat aroma and finesse, but is sometimes a little light. Under 3% of the vines in Alsace are of the Muscat variety and the wine is much in demand. It is pale in colour, with a pronounced, heady, 'musky' perfume yet with a dry finish. It is best drunk on its own, in order to appreciate the explosive but elegant aroma, or after a meal. A good Muscat is quite expensive but is worth the price and should always be drunk young. Price D–E.

Pinot Blanc

The Pinot Blanc is being planted more and more in Alsace, and has now reached 16% of the total under vines. The wines are fruity and dry, with a certain weight, but slightly lacking in finesse. They go very well with food and are generally very good value. Price C–D.

Pinot Noir

Red, but more usually rosé, wines are made from the Pinot Noir in Alsace. It is also vinified *en blanc* to make up the blend of Crémant d'Alsace. Only in sunny years are successful red wines made and, generally, Pinot Noir rosés are interesting as a change from the Alsace whites, rather than in themselves. Vinification is improving, however, leaving more the impression of strawberry Pinot Noir fruit than of alcohol. These wines should be served cool. The best come from Ottrott, near Obernai. Price D–E.

Riesling

The Riesling is the most noble of the *cépages nobles* planted in Alsace, and without doubt makes the finest wine. It is a wine of great elegance and style, with a fine, flowery bouquet, great depth of fruit on the palate and a marked lemony acidity that only enhances the flavour. The minor, less expensive Rieslings may be drunk young, but the finer wines are at their best at 3 to 8 years, and the finest examples, without even mentioning the extraordinary late-harvest wines, will improve for even longer. The soil on which Riesling provides the best wines is found around Ribeauvillé, Hunawihr and Ammerschwihr, but with proper ripening conditions, good Riesling can be made throughout the region. It is excellent with fresh-water fish, white meats and *coq au Riesling*. Price D–E–F.

Sylvaner

The Sylvaner accounts for just over 20% of the vines in Alsace. It makes a straightforward, light-coloured, refreshing wine with good acidity, different in taste, but fulfilling much the same role as Muscadet from the Loire. Like Muscadet, Sylvaner can also keep a slight *pétillance* if it is bottled very young. It gives of its best in the region of Barr, Rouffach and especially Mittelbergheim, from the Zotzenberg vineyard. It is a wine to drink young. Price C–D.

Tokay d'Alsace or Pinot Gris

Wines made from the Pinot Gris have habitually been sold under the name of Tokay d'Alsace, but owing to the confusion with the Hungarian Tokay, they must now be sold under the name of the *cépage*. The Pinot Gris represents not more than 5% of the vines planted in Alsace and makes a wine that is heavily perfumed, full-bodied and rich on the palate, low in acidity, but basically dry. It does not, however, have the spicy aroma of the Gewürztraminer or the elegant style of the Riesling. Wine which is made from the Pinot Gris grape is good with rich pâté, chicken and white meat, or can be drunk on its own. Good wines are made by the Cave Coopérative at Cleebourg and at Obernai and Kientzheim. Price D–E.

Alsace Grand Cru AOC

White wines only from the Riesling, Gewürztraminer, Pinot Gris (Tokay) and Muscat grapes, from certain specific vineyards in the Alsace wine region. The maximum yield is much lower than for the simple AOC Alsace, at 70 hl/ha, and the alcohol content before chaptalization must be 10° for the Rieslings and Muscats, 11° for the Gewürztraminers and Tokays. The wines are thus better structured and of intrinsically higher quality due to the siting of the vineyard. The name of the vineyard generally appears on the label, 'Riesling du Rangen' for example. The selection of Grand Cru vineyards is still expanding and does not tend to be used by the *négociants* or the very powerful Caves Coopératives, since their application is too limiting. In Alsace, better wines are differentiated from the lesser qualities by such words as *cuvée speciale, réserve personelle, réserve particulière* and so on. Price D–E.

Crémant d'Alsace AOC

White and a very little rosé sparkling wine made with Alsatian *vins de base* by the *méthode champenoise*. The Crémant rosé has to be made with wines from the Pinot Noir. The Crémants d'Alsace are good-quality sparkling wines, especially if the *vin de base* is the Pinot Blanc, but they are not in the same class as the Crémants which come from the Saône-et-Loire nor the *vins mousseux* from Vouvray. However, they do represent good value, and production is already over one million bottles. Price D.

Lorraine

The wines of Lorraine used to be highly esteemed and widely appreciated, but a succession of disasters for the *vignerons*, wars, the *phylloxera* and the more profitable business of planting plum trees, has reduced the vineyard area to 10% of what it was.

Côtes de Toul VDQS

Red, dry white, *gris* and rosé wines from vineyards planted around the city of Toul in the Meurthe-et-Moselle *département*. The vast majority of the production is of *vin gris*, a very pale rosé made almost exclusively from the Gamay. The Pinot Noir and Pinot Meunier are permitted, but are less and less planted. The *vin gris* is very light, with a minimum alcohol content of only 8.5° from a yield of 60 hl/ha, with an agreeable fruit and slight acidity that go very well with the local cuisine. The production is around 120,000 bottles, mostly drunk in the region. Price B.

Vins de Moselle VDQS

Red and dry white wines from what is left of the vineyards in the Moselle *département*. Red wines must be from the Gamay (to a minimum of 30%), the Pinot Noir and Pinot Gris, the whites from the Pinot Blanc and Sylvaner. They are light, the reds being pale in colour, although there are no rosés. In 1980, 3,600 bottles of red wine were produced and 1,300 bottles of white. Price C.

Vins de Pays

Vin de Pays de la Meuse

White and *gris* wines from a *département* that is more famous for its production of beer than wine. They are light and rather acidic and do not travel. Price A.

Burgundy

The vineyards of Burgundy extend across four *départements*
to the south-east of Paris: the Yonne, the Côte d'Or, the
Saône-et-Loire and the Rhône. In these *départements* there
are five wine regions: Chablis, the Côte d'Or (comprising
the Côte de Nuits and the Côte de Beaune), the Côte
Chalonnaise, the Mâconnais and the Beaujolais. With the
exception of Chablis, only 150 kilometres from Paris, an
enclave of vines disconnected from the rest of Burgundy by
a distance of 100 kilometres, there are vineyards with little
interruption from Dijon to Lyon.

For a region that is covered by a single name, Burgundy's wines are less homogeneous than, say, those of
Alsace or Champagne, but less diverse than those from the
Loire or the Rhône valleys. The immense variety of
appellations and *crus* come from two red grape varieties, the
Pinot Noir and the Gamay, and two white grapes, the
Chardonnay and the Aligoté. Of these four, Pinot Noir
and Chardonnay produce the finest wines. Pinot Noir is at
its best in the Côte d'Or: further north in the Yonne it
ripens well only in good years, while in the Mâconnais and
the Beaujolais to the south it makes a coarse, dull wine. Yet
in the centre of Burgundy its elegance is unsurpassed and
its variety infinite. Chardonnay adapts itself to the different soils and climate to make wines of characteristic style
and finesse throughout the Burgundy region. The Gamay
plays a minor role in the Côte d'Or and Côte Chalonnaise,
and comes into its own on the granite soil of the Beaujolais,
while the Aligoté, having no real character except crispness
and dryness, behaves in much the same way as the
Chardonnay.

From Chablis to Villefranche, these four grapes produce
a complete palette of wines – red, white, rosé and sparkling
– the difference between one wine and another lying in the
soil, the climate and the methods of wine-making.

The wines that have made the region's reputation world-
wide, the great red and white Burgundies from the Côte
d'Or, are beyond the scope of this book. There are,
however, many good local wines that are worth looking out
for, and each of the five main vineyards produces wines
which, if not in the everyday category, are affordable and
of excellent quality.

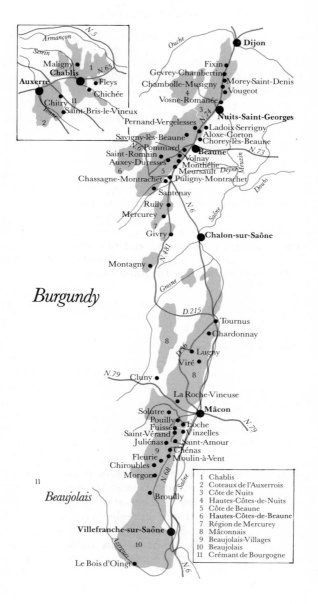

Armançon
Serein
N 5
Maligny
Chablis
1
N 65
Auxerre
Fleys
Chichée
11
Chitry
Saint-Bris-le-Vineux
Yonne
2

Ouche
Dijon
Fixin
Gevrey-Chambertin
Morey-Saint-Denis
Chambolle-Musigny
Vougeot
4
Vosne-Romanée
3
N 74
Nuits-Saint-Georges
Pernand-Vergelesses
Ladoix-Serrigny
Aloxe-Corton
Savigny-lès-Beaune
Chorey-lès-Beaune
N 73
N 6
Pommard
Beaune
Saint-Romain
Volnay
Auxey-Duresses
Monthélie
Deyne
Meuzin
6
5
Meursault
Chassagne-Montrachet
Puligny-Montrachet
Doubs
Santenay
Rully
N 6
Mercurey
Saône
7
Givry
Chalon-sur-Saône

N 481
Montagny

Grosne

Burgundy

D 215
Tournus
Chardonnay
8
D 6
Lugny
Viré
N 79
Cluny
8
La Roche-Vineuse
Solutré
Mâcon
Pouilly
Loché
N 79
Fuissé
Vinzelles
Saint-Vérand
Juliénas
Saint-Amour
9
Chénas
Fleurie
Moulin-à-Vent
Chiroubles
N 68
Morgon
Saône
11
Brouilly
Beaujolais
Villefranche-sur-Saône
10
Ardières
Le Bois d'Oingt
N 6

1	Chablis
2	Coteaux de l'Auxerrois
3	Côte de Nuits
4	Hautes-Côtes-de-Nuits
5	Côte de Beaune
6	**Hautes-Côtes-de-Beaune**
7	Région de Mercurey
8	Mâconnais
9	Beaujolais-Villages
10	Beaujolais
11	Crémant de Bourgogne

Regional or Generic Appellations

These basic *appellations* can be used throughout the Burgundy region, regardless of where the wine is made, so long as the accepted varietals are used. It is therefore most important for the consumer to see, from the label, where the wine is grown and bottled, as that information will point to the style of the wine. It is plain that a Bourgogne Aligoté or a Crémant de Bourgogne which is bottled in the Chablis region will be a very different wine from one of the same name bottled in the Mâconnais, the difference between them lying in the soil, the climate and possibly even the style of wine-making.

Bourgogne AOC

Red, white and rosé wines from the Burgundy wine region, covering specific areas in the *départements* of the Yonne, Côte d'Or, Saône-et-Loire and Rhône. The reds and rosés must be made from the Pinot Noir, with the exception of wines from the Mâconnais and the Beaujolais, where they may be from the Gamay, and from the Yonne, where the local grapes César and Tressot are permitted. The minimum alcohol content is 10° from a yield of 50 hl/ha. Bourgogne from the Pinot Noir, almost entirely from the Côte d'Or and the Côte Chalonnaise, should have all the qualities of the grape: a lovely cherry-ruby colour, not too dark, a strawberry-fruit aroma, with hints of blackcurrants, raspberries and wild cherries, the fruit carried through into a harmonious finish, neither too heavy, too acidic nor too sweet. The simple *appellation* Bourgogne (sometimes) lacks a definition of origin, if it is blended from the wines of several communes. If the wine is domaine-bottled, i.e. by the grower, it will state the origin on the label. Good examples of Bourgogne are very good value, and may be drunk relatively young at 2 to 6 years. Poorer examples will be evident from their too thin or too thick colour and lack of fruit and balance. Wines from any one or several of the 9 Beaujolais *crus* (see p. 51) may be declassified into Bourgogne, even though the wine is 100% from the Gamay grape. It is unfortunate that some Burgundy *négociants* use these wines to sell under the *appellation* Bourgogne, generally assumed to be from the Pinot Noir, yet it is still permitted by the INAO. Many Burgundy *négociants* add 'Pinot Noir' to the label of their Bourgognes if this is so.

White wines are made from the Chardonnay with sometimes some Pinot Blanc and Pinot Beurot, and must have a minimum alcohol content of 10.5°. The vast majority are pure Chardonnay from the Côte d'Or and the Côte Chalonnaise. They have a lovely pale greeny-gold colour, the appley-fruity Chardonnay aroma and a fullish flavour that finishes bone dry. They are a perfect introduction to the finer white Burgundies, and are best drunk with hors d'œuvres, fish and white meats and the local cheeses. Bourgogne rosé is not common, except in years of over-production like 1982. With its salmon-pink colour and delicate Pinot fruit, it is excellent with summer dishes. The *appellation* Bourgogne is usually good value. Price C–D.

Bourgogne Aligoté AOC

White wine from the Aligoté grape grown throughout the Burgundy region from Chablis to Villefranche-sur-Saône. Chardonnay is tolerated to a maximum of 15%, but the grapes are normally destined for Bourgogne blanc. Minimum alcohol content is 9.5° from a yield of 50 hl/ha. Bourgogne Aligoté is always pale in colour, crisp and dry with a tart finish. The style depends on where it is grown, crisper and lighter from around Chablis, for example, fruitier and fuller from Meursault. It is the perfect aperitif, the classic wine to mix with *crème de cassis* to make a Kir, or *vin blanc cassis*, and goes well with hors d'œuvres and fish. Aligoté should be drunk young and cold. Price C–D.

Bourgogne Clairet AOC

Rosé wines from the Burgundy region, made with the Pinot Noir. This *appellation* is very seldom seen, the wines being sold under the *appellation* Bourgogne Rosé. Price C–D.

Bourgogne Grand Ordinaire AOC

Red, white and rosé wines from the Burgundy region. This *appellation*, also known as Bourgogne Ordinaire, is the lowest on the Burgundy scale. Red wines may be made from the Pinot Noir, Gamay, and the César and Tressot if they are from the Yonne. Whites are from the Chardonnay, Pinot Blanc, Pinot Beurot, Aligoté, Melon de Bourgogne (the same grape as the Muscadet), and from the Sacy (Yonne). Minimum alcohol content must be 9.5°, from a yield of 50 hl/ha. The wines, mostly red, are unpretentious and fruity, but lack distinction. A few growers still make a BGO, as it is known, for local and Parisian clients. As there is little demand for BGOs, they tend to be genuine and seldom disappointing. It is worth trying it when in Burgundy, as very little is exported. Price C.

Bourgogne Passe-Tout-Grains AOC

Red (almost entirely) and rosé wines made principally in the Côte d'Or and the Côte Chalonnaise from a blend of not more than two-thirds Gamay and not less than one-third Pinot Noir. The alcohol content must exceed 9.5°, from a yield of 50 hl/ha. The best Passe-Tout-Grains are from the Côte de Beaune and the Côte de Nuits, where the percentage of Pinot is sometimes higher than the legal one-third. The wine is fruity, with a good colour, and is in general a very satisfying and slightly lighter alternative to Bourgogne. It should be drunk young, at 2 to 4 years, and may be served at cellar temperature. Bourgogne Passe-Tout-Grains is well worth looking out for. Price C(most)–D.

Bourgogne Rosé AOC

Rosé wines from the Burgundy region made from the Pinot Noir, with the César and Tressot permitted in wines from the Yonne. The minimum alcohol content must be 10°, from a maximum yield of 50 hl/ha. The Pinot Noir vinified as a rosé has a pretty salmon-pink colour, a light strawberry-Pinot aroma and a clean, fruity finish. It is at its best the summer after the vintage. Production varies greatly, as growers usually only produce a generic rosé, when they have a potential over-production of red wine. It is a wine to drink locally or in Parisian restaurants. Price C–D.

Crémant de Bourgogne AOC

White or rosé sparkling wine made from all the accepted Burgundy grapes, by the *méthode champenoise*. While this *appellation*, which has replaced that of Bourgogne Mousseux, covers the whole of Burgundy, the wines are fermented and bottled in their specific regions. Thus a Crémant de Bourgogne from the Yonne will be made from grapes grown in that region, and the same will apply to a Crémant from the Mâconnais. The Crémants de Bourgogne from the Côte Chalonnaise (particularly from Rully) and from the Mâconnais are the best. They have a fine *mousse* and are very elegant. The high proportion of Chardonnay (sometimes 100%) makes them a good alternative to a Blanc de Blancs from Champagne. They are also superb in a Kir Royal. The production of Crémant rosé is very small, that of Crémant blanc around 1.2 million bottles and in full expansion. Price D–E.

Chablis and North Burgundy

The vineyards of Chablis and the Auxerrois are the most northern in Burgundy, separated from the Côte d'Or by 150 kilometres. The soil is a limestoney-chalk, which gives Chablis more in common with Champagne than with the more clayey soil of central Burgundy. The white wines are crisp and dry, even slightly austere, with good fruit but none of the 'fleshiness' of the Chardonnays from further south. The production of reds and rosés has declined considerably, in favour of wines from sunnier climates.

Bourgogne Irancy AOC

Red and rosé wine from vineyards to the south-west of Chablis. Grapes planted are the Pinot Noir, and the local César and Tressot. The last two grape varieties are in the process of dying out. Wines from Irancy (which have to add Bourgogne to the label) must have a minimum alcohol content of 10° from a yield of 50 hl/ha. The wine was well known even in the twelfth century, but the popularity of wines from further south in Burgundy and then the phylloxera caused the production to fall to a mere 250,000 bottles today. In good years, Irancy red has a full, deep colour, a concentrated but slightly rustic fruitiness that softens well with age. In poor years, when the Pinot Noir does not ripen fully so far to the north, the Irancy rosé is a better bet, fresh and fruity, with a pleasant acidity. They are best drunk in the local restaurants. Price C – D.

Chablis AOC

White wine from the Chablis region in the Yonne *département* east of Auxerre. The only grape permitted is the Chardonnay, known locally as the Beaunois. It must have a minimum alcohol content of 10° from a yield of 40 hl/ha, both being exceeded in sunny or plentiful years. Chablis is pale yellow with a greeny tinge, a fine, lively distinctive bouquet, fills out with fruit on the palate and finishes bone dry. It may be drunk young, 1 or 2 years after the vintage, but ages remarkably well, better than most other white Burgundies. The finest wines are the Grands Crus and Premiers Crus, at their best only after 3 to 5 years. There has been much replanting in Chablis, and production is now around 6 million bottles. Chablis is perfect with shellfish, hors d'œuvres, river-fish and white meats. Drink chilled but not iced. The price from the growers is low in terms of other white Burgundies, and Chablis should be good value. Price D.

Petit Chablis AOC

White wine from the Chardonnay grape from anywhere in the Chablis region. Minimum alcohol content is only 9.5°, from a yield of 40 hl/ha, which is almost always exceeded. Petit Chablis comes usually from vines which are planted on the plains, or from vineyards in the outlying parts of the *appellation*. It is light and refreshing, with crisp, clean characteristic Chardonnay fruit. Petit Chablis is good value, and should be drunk at 1 to 3 years. Price D.

Sauvignon de Saint-Bris VDQS

White wine from the Sauvignon grape planted around the village of Saint-Bris-le-Vineux, to the south-west of Chablis. The wines are light (9.5° alcohol from a yield of 50 hl/ha), crisp and very dry, with the grassy, redcurranty Sauvignon fruit being toned down by the chalky soil and the northern exposition. Their high natural acidity makes the Sauvignon de Saint-Bris a good aperitif, especially in a Kir, and excellent with shellfish and hors d'œuvres. Drink very young. This is the only example of Sauvignon grown in Burgundy. Price B–C.

Côte d'Or
Côte de Nuits

The northern part of the Côte d'Or, comprising about 1,200 hectares running from the outskirts of Dijon in the north to Premeaux, south of Nuits-Saint-Georges. With very few exceptions, under 1% of the *appellation*, the wine produced is red, powerful but elegant, each commune having its own personality or style. From north to south, the communal *appellations* are: Fixin, Gevrey-Chambertin, Morey-Saint-Denis, Chambolle-Musigny, Vougeot, Vosne-Romanée and Nuits-Saint-Georges. From these vineyards come some of the finest wines in France and unquestionably the world's greatest wine from the Pinot Noir. None of the major *appellations*, with the possible exception of Fixin, is within the scope of this book.

Bourgogne Hautes-Côtes-de-Nuits AOC

Red, dry white and rosé wines from vineyards outside the *appellations communales* of the Côte de Nuits. Red and rosé wines must be made from the Pinot Noir, whites from the Chardonnay and Pinot Blanc. Minimum alcohol content is 10°, from a yield of 50 hl/ha. The white wines (only 5% of the *appellation*) are bouqueted and firm, really very good. The reds have a fine colour (in good years), good fruit and structure, and are typically slower to mature than the Hautes-Côtes-de-Beaune. They are at their best at 4 to 8 years. Production is around 850,000 bottles a year, and replanting is still continuing. With current prices in Burgundy, they represent good value. Price D.

Bourgogne Rosé de Marsannay AOC

Rosé wine from the commune of Marsannay-la-Côte, almost on the outskirts of Dijon. Made from the Pinot Noir, with a minimum alcohol content of 10° from a yield of

50 hl/ha, Rosé de Marsannay may also be known as Clairet de Marsannay. Pale salmon-pink in colour, with a delicate bouquet and all the characteristic fruit of the Pinot Noir on the palate, Rosé de Marsannay is reckoned, together with Tavel, to be the finest rosé in France. It is best drunk young, at 1 to 3 years, while it is still fresh and fruity, but is full-bodied enough to last longer. Price D.

Bourgogne Rouge de Marsannay AOC

Red wine from the Pinot Noir is made in the commune of Marsannay-la-Côte. Most of

the production is used for Rosé de Marsannay, but some growers produce a red, particularly in good years. The colour is generally lighter than other red wines from the Côte de Nuits, but the wine has good Pinot fruit and flavour and may be drunk relatively young at 3 to 5 years. Price D.

Côte de Nuits-Villages AOC

Red and dry white wines from five communes at the very north and very south of the Côte de Nuits: Brochon, Fixin, Comblanchien, Corgolin and Prissey. Minimum alcohol content is

10.5° for the reds, 11° for the whites, from a yield of 35 hl/ha. Production of white is infinitesimal, under 1,000 bottles, while that of red is considerable at around 1 million. The red has all the characteristics of a fine Côte de Nuits, and should be drunk at 5 to 10 years. They are much finer than the Hautes-Côtes-de-Nuits wines, with more fruit and texture, and they are the next best thing to the often over-priced *appellations communales*. Price E.

Fixin AOC

Red wine from the most northern *appellation communale* of the Côte de Nuits.

Minimum alcohol content 10.5°, yield 35 hl/ha. The wine may also be sold under the *appellation* Côte de Nuits-Villages. Fixin is a robust wine with many of the characteristics of Gevrey-Chambertin, but less finesse, at its best at 5 to 10 years. It is excellent with red meats and cheese, and is a very reliable wine, both in France and abroad. Price E.

Côte de Beaune

The southern half of the vineyards of the Côte d'Or, stretching from Ladoix in the north to Santenay in the south, covering an area of 2,800 hectares, over twice that of the Côte de Nuits. While the Côte de Nuits produces almost exclusively red wines, the Côte de Beaune produces white wines even more famous than its reds. Made from the Chardonnay grape grown in the communes of Corton, Meursault, Puligny-Montrachet and Chassagne-Montrachet, these are the finest dry white wines in France. The great red wines, with slightly more charm and softness than those from the Côte de Nuits, come from the following *appellations*: Aloxe-Corton, Pernand-Vergelesses, Savigny-lès-Beaune, Beaune, Pommard, Volnay, Monthélie, Blagny, Chassagne-Montrachet and Santenay. While these wines cannot be thought of as country wines, there do exist in the Côte de Beaune some *appellations* that are worth looking out for.

Auxey-Duresses AOC

Red and dry white wines from the commune of Auxey-Duresses to the west of Meursault. The red wines are from the Pinot Noir, with a minimum alcohol content of 10.5° from a yield of 35 hl/ha; the white wines are from the Chardonnay and Pinot Blanc

with an alcohol content of 11° from the same maximum yield. The whites are very good, in the style of a Montrachet in a minor, more discreet, key, with a lovely pale yellow robe, the distinctive Chardonnay flavour and some finesse. The reds have a good ruby colour, are smooth and elegant and quite quick maturing. Production is around 550,000 bottles of red annually, 180,000 of white. They are both good examples of the Côte de Beaune. Price E.

Bourgogne Hautes-Côtes-de-Beaune AOC

Red, dry white and rosé wines from vineyards outside (and, as the name implies, higher in elevation than) the *appellation* Côte de Beaune. Reds and rosés are from the Pinot Noir grape, whites from the Chardonnay and Pinot Blanc. The wines must have a minimum alcohol content of 10°, from a maximum yield of 50 hl/ha. This relatively new *appellation* produces red wines with good colour, fruit and personality that are less complex and velvety than the more expensive wines from the Côte de Beaune *appellation*. There has been much replanting of vines and the growers are very serious. Production is around 1.3 million bottles, of which 98% is red. Good value for money, especially in good years. Price C–D.

Cheilly-lès-Maragnes AOC
Dezize-lès-Maragnes AOC
Sampigny-lès-Maragnes AOC

These three villages, just inside the Saône-et-Loire *département*, make red wine from the Pinot Noir that has the right to be sold either under the village name, or that of Côte de Beaune-Villages. The latter *appellation* is more popular. These are well-made, fruity wines that should be drunk relatively young. Price D–E.

Chorey-lès-Beaune AOC

Red wines from the north of the Côte de Beaune, on the other side of the RN 74 from Aloxe-Corton. Made from the Pinot Noir, with a minimum alcohol content of 10.5° from a yield of 35 hl/ha (which is often exceeded), Chorey-lès-Beaune is a well-made, sturdy wine, which is often sold under the more popular *appellation* of Côte de Beaune-Villages. Even though the wines come from the plain, they have distinction and are good value for money. Annual production is around 600,000 bottles. Price E.

Côte de Beaune-Villages AOC

Red wines from one or more specific communes in the Côte de Beaune, made from the Pinot Noir. They must have a minimum alcohol content of 10.5°, from a maximum yield of 35 hl/ha, although this is often exceeded in big vintages. The wines have a velvety-ruby colour, and are attractively fruity with some finesse. Although they are more anonymous than the wines from individual communes, they are generally good value. Drink at 3 to 8 years, with *charcuterie*, poultry, red meats and cheese. Price E.

Saint-Aubin AOC

Red and dry white wines from vineyards in the hills to the south-east of Beaune, near le Rochepot. The reds, from the Pinot Noir, are light and fruity with a lot of style; the whites, from the Chardonnay, are generally considered to be superior, with fine flowery taste and elegant finish. Both may be drunk young, even the red, at 2 to 4 years. While many *négociants* buy these wines to sell under the label of Côte de Beaune-Villages, those growers who are bottling their own wine under the Saint-Aubin *appellation* are very proud of their wine and justly convinced of its quality. Price E.

Saint-Romain AOC

Red and dry white wines from vineyards on the high slopes to the east of Beaune. Grape varieties permitted are the Pinot Noir for the reds and the Chardonnay and Pinot Blanc for the whites, both subject to the same rules of *appellation* as Côte de Beaune-Villages, under which name they may be sold. Owing to the elevation, the wines are often subject to frost, particularly the early-budding Chardonnay. Saint-Romain blanc is fine and lively, with a firm acidity that allows it to last well. The reds have an excellent colour, a firm Pinot aroma and a certain earthiness in the finish. They are at their best from 4 to 8 years. Saint-Romain wines lack something of the charm and suppleness of the Côte de Beaune style, but are good value. Price E.

Côte Chalonnaise

The most southern part of the central vineyards, named after the town of Chalon-sur-Saône. The grapes are the same as in the Côte d'Or: Pinot Noir for reds and rosés, Chardonnay (with Pinot Blanc still permitted) for the whites. The Aligoté grape makes a very fine Bourgogne Aligoté, and the Gamay is used for Bourgogne Passe-Tout-Grains and Bourgogne Grand Ordinaire. The Côte Chalonnaise has five *appellations* (see below), apart from making some very successful Bourgogne rouge from the Pinot Noir, and some of the best Crémant de Bourgogne. An *appellation* Côte Chalonnaise is under discussion by the INAO for wines of superior quality from Pinot Noir and Chardonnay planted exclusively in the Côte Chalonnaise.

Bourgogne Aligoté de Bouzeron AOC

Dry white wine from the Aligoté grape grown in the commune of Bouzeron, just outside the town of Chagny.

The village of Bouzeron was recently awarded its own *appellation* of Bourgogne Aligoté (see page 37), owing to the particular quality of the Aligoté wines from this area. They are usually bottled in the spring following the vintage and may be drunk straight away for their delicious fruit and crisp acidity. Well worth looking out for in the local restaurants. Price D.

Givry AOC

Red and dry white wines from vineyards in the middle of the Côte Chalonnaise, directly to the east of Chalon-sur-Saône. The red wines, from the Pinot Noir, are like Mercurey, but generally with less depth and complexity. The lighter years may be drunk young, at 2 years, and even served cool to enhance the fruit. The whites, from the Chardonnay, with half a degree more alcohol at 11.5° from a yield of 40 hl/ha, are pale, fruity and firm, not unlike a light Meursault. Most of the small production of white is drunk locally, while the red has acquired a reputation in Paris and northern Europe. Well worth looking for. Price D.

Mercurey AOC

Red and dry white wines from the north of the Côte Chalonnaise. Before the laws of *appellation*, these wines, made from the Pinot Noir and the Chardonnay, were grouped with those from the Côte de Beaune. The reds, representing 95% of the production, an average of 3 million bottles, must have a minimum alcohol content of 10.5° (11° for the *premiers crus*), from a maximum yield of 35 hl/ha. They have a fine colour, a fruity, often blackcurranty, bouquet and a firm but elegant taste. They may be drunk at 3 to 5 years, but should be kept much longer in good years, and are particularly good with chicken, red meats and cheese. The very small production of white wine is crisp and fine, sometimes a little acidic when young, an interesting curiosity. The red is good value. Price E.

Montagny AOC

Dry white wine from the Chardonnay grape grown in the vicinity of Buxy in the south of the Côte Chalonnaise. Montagny must have a minimum alcohol content of 11.5° from a yield of 40 hl/ha and is, after Rully, the best white wine from the region. It is pale yellow in colour, with lots of fruit and a stylish, dry finish, mid-way between the wines from the Côte de Beaune and those from the Mâconnais. It is very good with hors d'œuvres, excellent with fish and white meats. Production is around 300,000 bottles annually, with very good wine from the Coopérative at Buxy and the better growers. Price D.

Rully AOC

Red and dry white wines from the communes of Rully and Chagny. The white, from the Chardonnay and Pinot Blanc, is the better known. Minimum alcohol content is 11° (11.5° for the *premiers crus*), from a yield of 40 hl/ha. A good Rully blanc with its pale golden colour, Chardonnay bouquet of fruit touched with green apples and fresh almonds, and stylish finish is the equal of many more prestigious wines from the Côte de Beaune. Rully rouge, from the Pinot Noir, has a light ruby colour, a fruity bouquet and a firm, clean finish and may be drunk at 2 years. The chalky soil also produces wines of a finesse that makes them particularly good as Crémant de Bourgogne. Over-all good, some excellent. Price D–E.

The Mâconnais

The region called the Mâconnais stretches from a little north of Tournus to just south of Mâcon, an area about 35 kilometres long and 10 to 15 kilometres wide, in the Saône-et-Loire *département*. The vines, which are planted in soil with a granite base and some limestone, are all to be found on the left bank of the river Saône. The total area under vines is around 6,000 hectares, very much less than in the days before phylloxera, but there is encouraging expansion at the present time. The Chardonnay grape (with some Pinot Blanc) accounts for almost 60% of the total, Gamay 30%, Pinot Noir 10% with a little Aligoté. A very high proportion of the production – 70% – is handled by the Caves Coopératives, whose wine is of a consistently high quality. Apart from the well-known Mâcon *appellations*, a great deal of Bourgogne blanc (Chardonnay) is produced, Bourgogne rouge, Bourgogne Passe-Tout-Grains, Bourgogne Grand Ordinaire, a little Bourgogne Aligoté and a great deal of excellent Crémant de Bourgogne. The finest wines from the Mâconnais region are to be found at Pouilly-Fuissé.

Mâcon (blanc) or Pinot-Chardonnay-Mâcon AOC

White wine from the Mâconnais, made from the Chardonnay grape, with the Pinot Blanc permitted, but playing a smaller and smaller role. The wine must have a minimum alcohol content of 10°, from a maximum basic yield of 50 hl/ha. Mâcon blanc is the lightest of the white Mâconnais wines, pale primrose yellow, clean, fresh and fruity with an attractive acidity. It should be drunk within 2 years of the vintage with hors d'œuvres, *charcuterie*, fish or poultry, or just on its own, served cold. Good value. Price C.

Mâcon (Blanc) Supérieur AOC

Dry white wine from the Mâconnais, similar in every way to Mâcon blanc, except that the wine must have a degree more alcohol at 11°, hence more body and fruit. This *appellation* is being superseded by the better-sounding Mâcon-Villages. Good value in plentiful years. Price D.

Mâcon (Rouge or Rosé) AOC

Red and rosé wines from the Mâconnais. The grapes used are the Gamay, Pinot Noir with Pinot Gris permitted but seldom seen, and the wines must have a minimum of 9° alcohol from a yield of 50 hl/ha. They are attractive everyday wines, usually light in colour, without too much body and flavour. Best drunk on the spot. Price C.

Mâcon Supérieur Rouge (or Rosé) AOC

Red and rosé wines from the Mâconnais, with one degree more alcohol than Mâcon rouge. Red Mâcon may be made either from the Gamay or the Pinot Noir – if it is a mix of these two grapes it must be of a minimum of one-third Pinot Noir, and is called Bourgogne Passe-Tout-Grains – and the wine tends to resemble either a Beaujolais or a rather rustic Bourgogne. The wines have a deep cherry colour, a good deal of fruit, but are never very smooth. They are best drunk with food, *charcuterie*, poultry, red meats and cheese at 1 to 4 years after the vintage. Mâcon rosés have a pretty violetty-pink colour and should be drunk young, while still fresh, served cold. Even the reds may be served cool. Annual production is around 8 million bottles. Since the neighbouring Beaujolais are much more popular, Mâcon rouge is often ignored, and is usually good value. Price C.

Mâcon-Villages or Mâcon followed by the name of a commune AOC

Dry white wine from the Mâconnais with rules as for Mâcon Supérieur. Mâcon-Villages is the most commercialized of the white Mâcons and represents 11 million of the 14 million bottles produced annually. It is a classic Chardonnay type: pale yellow, with flowery, appley aromas, a strikingly fruity taste and enough body to enhance the flavour without making the wine too serious.

A good Mâcon-Villages should have a refreshing acidity, perfect for drinking on its own, or with food, preferably *charcuterie* and river-fish. The name of any of 43 communes may be added to the word Mâcon to replace Villages (which is generally a blend of more than one commune) if the wine is from that village alone. The best known are: Clessé, Fuissé, Igé, Lugny, Prissé, Viré and Uchizy. Eighty per cent of the production is handled by Caves Coopératives, of which Lugny and Viré are particularly good. Except in years when the quantity of wine made is much reduced by weather conditions and short supply pushes prices up, Mâcon-Villages is very good value. Price D.

Pouilly-Fuissé *AOC*

Dry white wine from the
Mâconnais, made exclusively
from the Chardonnay planted
in the communes of Fuissé,
Solutré, Pouilly, Vergisson
and Chaintré. The wine must
have a minimum alcohol
content of 11° (12° if the name
of the vineyard is mentioned),
from a maximum yield of 45
hl/ha. Pouilly-Fuissé is
without doubt the finest wine
of the Mâconnais, a
Chardonnay of great class, on
a par with a Meursault or a
good Chablis. The colour is
pale gold, with green lights,
the bouquet subtle but
distinctive, the taste rich and
complex, but completely dry.
It is a wine generally exciting
and very satisfying, and
should be drunk at a
minimum of 3 years after the
vintage, improving for 5 to 8
years more. Pouilly-Fuissé
should not be confused with
Pouilly-Fumé, from the Loire.
It is at its best with river-fish
or chicken. Even the average
production of 4 million bottles
is not enough to satisfy
demand, and it is always quite
expensive. Price F.

Pouilly-Loché *AOC*

The same style of dry white
wine as Pouilly-Fuissé, from
the commune of Loché. They
do not match the quality of
Pouilly-Fuissé, but are less
expensive. Only 150,000
bottles are produced a year,
mostly drunk on the spot or
bought by a French clientele.
Price E.

Pouilly-Vinzelles *AOC*

Dry white wine similar to
Pouilly-Loché, from the
commune of Vinzelles and
part of Loché. The next best
thing to Pouilly-Fuissé. Better
known than Pouilly-Loché,
with an average production of
270,000 bottles. Price E.

Saint-Véran *AOC*

Dry white wine from the
Mâconnais, made exclusively
from the Chardonnay grape,
grown in seven communes
surrounding Fuissé. This
newly created *appellation*
(1971) must have a minimum
of 11° alcohol from a
maximum yield of 45 hl/ha,
the same as the wines of
Pouilly. Saint-Véran is very
similar in style, a classic
Chardonnay of finesse,
vitality and distinction. It is
very good in the year
following the vintage, but is at
its best at 2 to 5 years old with
charcuterie or river-fish.
Production is almost 2 million
bottles annually, and in price
it is much nearer to a Mâcon-
Villages than to a Pouilly-
Fuissé. Very good value. Price
D – E.

The Beaujolais

The Beaujolais is the most southern vineyard area of Burgundy and is also the largest, covering about 15,000 hectares, most of them in the Rhône *département*. The region is probably also the prettiest in Burgundy, with vines intermingled with red-roofed farm buildings, covering the valleys and hills up to a height of 500–600 metres, completely dominating the Saône Valley. The principal grape planted is the Gamay, which comes into its own in the granite-based soil of the Beaujolais. Further north in Burgundy, in the Côte d'Or, the Gamay produces a dullish wine, and only in Touraine does it make wines anywhere near as fruity as those in the Beaujolais. The best wines, the Villages and the *crus*, come from the north; those from the south, an area known as 'Beaujolais Bâtard', are lighter and are generally sold *en primeur*. There is a little Chardonnay planted to the north, in the Saône-et-Loire *département*, whose wines resemble those of the Mâconnais. Average annual production of Beaujolais, red, white and rosé, is about 150 million bottles.

Beaujolais *AOC*

Red, dry white and rosé wines from vineyards in the Saône-et-Loire *département* south of Mâcon and the Rhône *département* north of Lyon. The reds and rosés are from the Gamay grape, the whites from the Chardonnay. Pinot Noir, Pinot Gris and Aligoté grapes are permitted in theory, but in fact are not used for Beaujolais. Reds and rosés must have a minimum alcohol content of 9°, whites of 9.5° from a yield of 50 hl/ha (almost always exceeded). The wines are light, fruity, quaffable, the perfect *vin de carafe*. Over 90% of the *appellation* is red, a little under half of all Beaujolais produced, and should always be drunk under one year old, served cool. Beaujolais, especially the Beaujolais Primeur that is released for sale on 15 November, only a few weeks after the vintage, should have a pretty violetty-red colour, an attractive grapey nose and a fresh fruity taste. It is a simple, cheerful drink. Price C.

Beaujolais Supérieur *AOC*

Red, dry white and rosé wines conforming to the same rules as Beaujolais, with a higher minimum alcohol content of 10°. White wines represent under 5% of the 2 million or so bottles declared annually, and the production of rosé is insignificant. This is an old-fashioned *appellation*, not seen outside France. The wines very much resemble Beaujolais *tout court*, but may be kept a little longer. Price C.

Beaujolais-Villages AOC

Red, dry white and rosé wines from the Gamay and Chardonnay grapes grown in the northern part of the Beaujolais region. Production of white is minute, much of what is made being sold under the Saint-Véran *appellation*, although Beaujolais blanc is worth looking out for. Rosé tends to be drunk up locally. The red Villages wines are fruity, charming, and can be quite full-bodied, while losing nothing of their quaffability. In terms of quality, they are only slightly less good than the *crus*, and represent the best value for money in the Beaujolais. Drink preferably in the first year after the vintage, although good vintages may keep for a year longer. Price C.

The Beaujolais Crus

The northern part of the Beaujolais region, previously known as the Haut-Beaujolais, is possessed of 9 *crus*, or single-village wines, each of which may sell under its own name. They are exclusively red, made from the Gamay, and must have a minimum alcohol content of 10° (11° if a vineyard or *climat* name is specified), from a maximum yield of 50 hl/ha. In practice, the degrees, aided by chaptalization (see page 12), are usually in the range of 12.5–13.5°, but the wines have a corresponding depth of fruit that some Beaujolais or Beaujolais-Villages do not possess. According to their lightness or intensity of flavour, the various *crus* go very well with *charcuterie*, veal, chicken (especially *coq au vin*), red meats, game and cheese. They can, of course, be drunk on their own, and should be served at cellar temperature (12°C).

Brouilly AOC

The largest of the *crus*, covering over 1,000 hectares around Odenas and Saint-Lager, producing more than 8 million bottles. It is a typical Beaujolais, fruity, soft and charming, with a lovely bouquet and inviting quality characteristic of the Gamay grape. At its best very young, as it does not improve with age. Very good value. Price C.

Chénas AOC

Deep, ruby-coloured wine from a *cru* whose wine is often overlooked, owing to the presence of Moulin-à-Vent's adjacent vineyards. Chénas is a well-built, generous wine, with an attractive floral nose (peonies) and an elegant fruit finish. It is less charming than Brouilly, less stylish than Fleurie or Chiroubles, but very enjoyable and ages well. It is well worth looking out for. Price D.

Chiroubles AOC

Situated between Fleurie and Morgon, Chiroubles is one of the lighter *crus*, but one of the most stylish. The wines are much in demand in France, where they are drunk in the spring following the vintage. A good Chiroubles is Beaujolais at its best. Scarcity has created a highish price. Price D–E.

Côte-de-Brouilly AOC

At the centre of the Brouilly *appellation*, Côte-de-Brouilly comes from vines on the steep slopes of the Montagne-de-Brouilly. It is tougher and firmer than Brouilly, but opens up with a depth of bouquet (violets) and taste that Brouilly lacks. Can be drunk young, or kept for 2 to 3 years. Price D.

Fleurie AOC

A very attractive and stylish wine, known as the 'Queen of the Beaujolais', Fleurie has a good colour, a beautifully flowery bouquet and a harmonious, elegant finish. It is best drunk within 18 months of the vintage, but wines from old vines or good years can age longer. It is one of the more expensive *crus*, but worth it. Price D–E.

Juliénas AOC

Deep, purple-coloured wine from vineyards at the north tip of the Rhône *département*. This sturdy wine has a surprisingly elegant bouquet of raspberries and *pêches de vigne*, and the combination makes Juliénas one of the loveliest wines of the region. It may be drunk young, 6 months after the vintage, to appreciate the stunning fruit, or kept for 2 to 4 years. Usually the same price as Morgon, and good value. Price D.

Morgon *AOC*

The second-largest production, after Brouilly, Morgon is a big, meaty wine compared to Fleurie or Chiroubles. It has a deep ruby colour and a richness of flavour that develops best after 1 to 2 years in bottle. When young, it has less of the Beaujolais fruit than the other *crus*, but can develop an almost Burgundian character with age. Morgon is justifiably popular with wine-drinkers who want more than just the Gamay taste. Among the *crus*, Morgon represents good value. Price D.

Moulin-à-Vent *AOC*

Deep-coloured and famous red wines from the communes of Romanèche-Thorins and Chénas, Moulin-à-Vent is the most prestigious of the *crus*. It should always have a deep colour, with the fruit of the Gamay underlined by a velvety richness. Moulin-à-Vent can be drunk young, in the year following the vintage, a huge mouthful of wine, but many of the other *crus* are at their best then; in good vintages it comes into its own after 3 years, and can last 10 years or more. It is the most expensive of the *crus*. Price E.

Saint-Amour *AOC*

The furthest north of the Beaujolais *crus*, entirely in the Saône-et-Loire *département*, Saint-Amour is often lighter in colour than the others, but quite firm on the palate. While it is a very good Beaujolais, it seems to lack any outstanding quality. Its name is not ineffective in making it one of the more expensive *crus*. Price D–E.

Adjacent Vineyards

Coteaux du Lyonnais *VDQS*

Red, dry white and rosé wines from vineyards to the south of Villefranche-sur-Saône and around Lyon in the Rhône *département*. The reds and rosés, over 95% of the production, are from the Gamay, producing a wine like Beaujolais, a little less lively, but with a genuine *goût de terroir*. The whites can be from the Chardonnay, Aligoté and Melon de Bourgogne, and are crisp, fruity and dry. They are all drunk on the spot. Production is over a million bottles, and the wines are popular in bistros in Lyon and Paris. Very enjoyable and inexpensive. Price B.

Vins de Pays

Vin de Pays de l'Yonne

White wines from the region of Chablis, Irancy, Coulanges-la-Vineuse and Saint-Bris. The grapes may be Chardonnay, Aligoté, Sacy or Sauvignon, with a maximum yield of 80 hl/ha and a minimum alcohol content of 9°. Very light, crisp, dry, even rather tart wines, the best from the Chardonnay on its own. Price A.

The Rhône Valley

The vineyards of the Côtes du Rhône follow the Rhône river from Vienne to Avignon for nearly 200 kilometres. In common with the Loire Valley, this region offers the most diverse selection of wines possible; dry white wines, rich *demi-sec* whites, rosés, light red wines, heavy red wines, sparkling wines and even *vins doux naturels*. If there is a common theme, it is perhaps the intensity of flavour, a certain definitiveness between the different *appellations*. The sun is ever-present and yet Rhône wines do not suffer from the uniformity often found in wines from hot climates.

The vineyards are clearly divided into two regions: the Côtes du Rhône Septentrionales in the north and the Côtes du Rhône Méridionales in the south. Wines are also produced in the middle, but much of this is quite recent. The style of wine will depend as much on the proportion of grapes as on the soil, as is evident from the wines themselves. The Grenache, dominant except in the north, gives big colour and body; Syrah (totally dominant in the north) brings a dark, purply robe and a firm spicy flavour; Cinsault, especially useful in *vins rosés*, tempers the rich fruit of the Grenache with a slightly tart elegance; and Mourvèdre, a difficult, low-yielding varietal, gives the wine structure and ageing potential. Vines in the north tend to be planted in steeply terraced vineyards on both sides of the river, while in the south they are to be found mostly on the dry, arid plains. In general, wines from the north tend to be firmer and less rich in alcohol.

The Rhône is thought of as a red-wine region in the same way as the Loire is considered white-wine country. This exclusiveness is more true of the Rhône, where white and rosés account for less than 10% of the *appellation*. With two notable exceptions, Condrieu (and Château Grillet) and Hermitage from the north, the Rhône does not produce white wine to rival the great wines from Alsace, Burgundy and the Loire. The most interesting white from the southern Rhône is actually not a table wine at all, but a *vin doux naturel*, the Muscat de Beaumes-de-Venise. Throughout the last decade, all Rhône wines have been gaining in popularity. This is due partly to wine-drinkers moving away from the established names, but more so to the efforts of the growers, Caves Coopératives and *négociants* to improve the quality and retain the individuality of their wines. The hoardings along the *autoroute du sud* still announce 'Côtes du Rhône, Vins du Soleil'. They are much more than that.

1	Côtes du Rhône
1a	Côtes du Rhône-Villages
2	Côte-Rôtie
3	Condrieu
4	Château Grillet
5	Hermitage
5a	Crozes-Hermitage
6	Saint-Joseph
7	Cornas
8	Saint-Péray
9	Châteauneuf-du-Pape
10	Lirac
11	Tavel
12	Beaumes-de-Venise
13	Gigondas
14	Rasteau

15	Clairette de Die
16	Coteaux du Tricastin
17	Côtes du Ventoux
18	Côtes du Luberon

Côtes du Rhône

Côtes du Rhône AOC

Red, dry white and rosé wines from grapes planted on both sides of the Rhône Valley, from Vienne in the north to Avignon in the south, covering the *départements* of the Rhône, Loire, Drôme, Ardèche, Gard and the Vaucluse. This *appellation* covers 80% of all wines produced in the Rhône Valley. The red wines and the small quantity of rosés are made from a minimum of 70% *cépages nobles*: Grenache, Syrah, Mourvèdre and Cinsault, with the addition of the lesser-known Counoise,

Muscardin, Vaccarèse, Terret Noir and Camarèse, and a maximum of 30% Carignan, the high-producing grape from the Midi.

For all wines bearing the Côtes du Rhône *appellation*, minimum alcohol content must be 11°, from a yield of 50 hl/ha. White wines must be made from the Clairette, Roussanne, Marsanne, Grenache Blanc and Bourboulenc grapes, with a little Ugni Blanc. These are generally pleasant and fruity, yet all but the best lack acidity, and should definitely be drunk up in the year after the vintage, before they lose their freshness. They go well with the local food and climate. Rosés are often too high in alcohol to be really refreshing, and should always be drunk young and cold. Even the red Côtes du Rhône *génériques* are best drunk at 1 to 3 years, and in hot weather should be served cool to lower the impression of alcohol and to enhance the fruit. Average production is about 200 million bottles of red and rosé, 3 million bottles of white. Most of this is produced by Caves Coopératives. Côtes du Rhône is generally very good value, but there are still some poor wines made. Price B.

Côtes du Rhône-Villages AOC

Red, dry white and rosé wines from 17 specific communes in the Vaucluse, Gard and southern Drôme *départements*. All Côtes du Rhône-Villages come from the southern part of the valley and are discussed on page 62.

The Northern Rhône Valley

The vineyards that are called in France the Côtes du Rhône Septentrionales stretch from Vienne to Valence in a narrow strip, following the river Rhône. In marked contrast to the Côtes du Rhône Méridionales in the south, where the vineyards tend to occupy the plain, here vines are planted on terraced slopes dominating the valley. The Syrah is the principal grape, producing the excellent wines of Hermitage and Côte-Rôtie, two of the finest wines in France. Côte-Rôtie, quite exceptionally, may use up to 20% of a white grape, the Viognier, a very rare varietal that is planted only around Ampuis and Condrieu. There is some very good simple Côtes du Rhône made from vines planted on the right bank of the Rhône, in the region of Saint-Désirat, as well as on the plain to the east of Tain-l'Hermitage.

Cornas AOC

Red wine only from around the village of Cornas in the Ardèche *département*, south of Tournon on the right bank of the Rhône. Here the only grape is the Syrah, and Cornas is the Syrah at its most extreme: very deep, almost black in colour, with a rich heady aroma of concentrated fruit (blackcurrants, raspberries, violets), a rough wine when young which softens out wonderfully after 5 years. Minimum alcohol content is 10.5°, from a yield of 40 hl/ha, but the actual yield is generally lower, as the vines are almost all *en coteaux*, resulting in a wine more naturally concentrated. Less noble than Hermitage, less elegant than Côte-Rôtie, Cornas is the next best thing. It is wonderful with red meats, stews and game. Production is relatively low, and Cornas is rarely, if ever, disappointing. Price E.

Crozes-Hermitage AOC

Red and dry white wines from vineyards around the town of Tain-l'Hermitage in the Drôme *département*. The red wine must be made from the Syrah grape (although up to 15% white grapes from the *appellation* may be added during fermentation, this no longer happens, as the white wine sells well on its own). Minimum alcohol content must be 11°, from a maximum yield of 40 hl/ha.

Red Crozes-Hermitage has a lovely deep cherry-ruby colour, violetty-purple when young, an aroma of blackcurrants or raspberries and a smooth, spicy fruit. Yet with few exceptions, it should not be classed, as it sometimes is, as a minor Hermitage. It is at its best drunk 2 to 5 years after the vintage. The white wine is made from the Roussanne and the Marsanne grapes, mostly Marsanne, as the Roussanne is so low-yielding. It is pale yellow in colour, with an acacia aroma, good fruit and an intentionally crisp finish. It goes very well as an aperitif, with hors d'œuvres such as smoked ham and melon, or with fish. The red Crozes-Hermitage is good with chicken, red meats and game. Production is increasing, and now stands at 4.5 million bottles of red, 500,000 of white. Some grower's wines are quite excellent. Price C – D.

Saint-Joseph AOC

Red and dry white wines from vines planted on the right (west) bank of the Rhône, around Tournon and Mauves in the Ardèche *département*. The grapes are the same as for Crozes-Hermitage: Syrah for the reds, mostly Marsanne for the white, with a maximum yield of 40 hl/ha and a required minimum of 10° alcohol. The white wines have great finesse, with a subtle aroma of apricots, and are strikingly elegant, almost as good as Hermitage blanc, with the advantage that they can be drunk young. Unfortunately, demand outstrips supply and they are quite rare. Red Saint-Joseph is deep-coloured, generally firmer and more rustic than Crozes-Hermitage, often needing 3 years to develop, and can last 8. The reds are less expensive than the whites. Price D – E.

Saint-Péray AOC

Dry white wine from opposite Valence on the right bank of the Rhône. Grapes are the Roussanne and the Marsanne, making a pale, straw-coloured wine, with an aroma of violets and a lively natural acidity. It may be drunk young, or kept. Most of the production is drunk locally or sold to private clients but its distinctive style certainly makes it worth looking for. Price D.

Saint-Péray Mousseux AOC

Sparkling wine from the Saint-Péray vineyards opposite Valence on the right bank of the Rhône. The *vin tranquille* is made sparkling by the *méthode champenoise*. Saint-Péray Mousseux was once the most famous sparkling wine in France after Champagne. It is more golden in colour than Champagne and has more body, because of the grape varieties planted and the climate. More sparkling wine than still wine is produced. Price D – E.

The Middle Côtes du Rhône

Between the easily defined areas of the Côtes du Rhône Septentrionales and Méridionales lie vineyards covering the *départements* of the Drôme and the Ardèche. There has been much replanting in this middle area, particularly in the Tricastin *appellation* between Montélimar and Bollène, but the main form of agriculture remains fruit-growing. Apart from the *appellations* cited below, there is some soft, fruity Côtes du Rhône made south of Valence around la Voulte-sur-Rhône on the right bank and Livron-sur-Drôme on the left.

Châtillon-en-Diois AOC

Red, dry white and rosé wines from vineyards on the left bank of the Rhône in the Drôme *département* south and east of Die. Reds and rosés must be from a minimum of 75% Gamay and a maximum of 25% Syrah and Pinot Noir. They are light in alcohol, with a minimum of 11° from a maximum yield of 50 hl/ha, quite light in colour and body, fruity and should be drunk young. The whites, about 10% of the *appellation*, are from the Burgundy grapes Chardonnay and Aligoté, light and lively for a wine of this region. Almost all the production comes from the Caves Coopératives. Although inexpensive, the quality is not much better than a good vin de pays. Price B.

Clairette de Die AOC

Dry and *demi-sec* sparkling wine from around Die on both banks of the river Drôme, to the west of Valence. Grape varieties planted are the Clairette and the Muscat à Petits Grains. The still wines, made exclusively from the Clairette, are crisp and lively, but the emphasis is on the sparkling wine. For this, two methods are used: the *méthode champenoise*, using wines principally from the Clairette, and sold as Clairette de Die brut, and the *méthode dioise* (or *méthode rurale*, similar to the *méthode gaillaçoise*, page 169), dealing with wines generally with at least 50% Muscat, and sold as Clairette de Die demi-sec or Tradition. The latter wine is much superior with a less aggressive sparkle and the bouquet of the Muscat completely preserved. Clairette de Die Mousseux is best drunk young, on its own or with desserts, served very cold. The Cave Coopérative produces three-quarters of the annual 6 million bottles, the Cuvée Tradition being the best. Price D.

Coteaux du Tricastin AOC

Red, dry white and rosé wines from vineyards to the east of the Rhône, between Montélimar and Bollène in the Drôme *département*. Tricastin has been the fastest-growing vineyard in the Côtes du Rhône, receiving VDQS status in 1964 from nothing ten years before and full *appellation* status ten years later. The grapes planted are the classic Rhône varieties, with about 50–60% Grenache, 20% Syrah, the rest being made up of Cinsault, Mourvèdre and Carignan. The reds resemble the deep-coloured soft fruity Côtes du Rhône from the south, with a satisfying spiciness and liveliness from the Syrah. The rosés are pleasant, and the small quantity of white (all consumed on the spot) is full and flavourful. Minimum alcohol content is 11°, from a yield of 50 hl/ha. The red is the best of the Tricastin wines, representing excellent value. Price C.

Côtes du Vivarais VDQS

Red, dry white and rosé wines from vineyards on the west bank of the Rhône, in the Ardèche and northern Gard *départements*, above Pont-Saint-Esprit. Grapes planted are the same as for the Côtes du Rhône *génériques*, with the Gamay admitted. The production of white is tiny, under 1% of the total of almost 3 million bottles. The reds and rosés are fruity and easy to drink, perhaps lighter and more acidic than the Côtes du Rhône. They are perfect wines to drink when on holiday in the Ardèche. Price B.

Haut-Comtat VDQS

Red and rosé wines from at least 50% Grenache, planted to the east of the Rhône, around Nyons in the Drôme *département*. These solid, well-made wines are not seen any more, as they mostly sell under the Côtes du Rhône *appellation* from the villages of Saint-Pantaléon-les-Vignes and Rousset (see page 64). Price C.

The Southern Côtes du Rhône

The Côtes du Rhône Méridionales occupy land on either side of the Rhône, between Pont-Saint-Esprit and Avignon, stretching across the *départements* of the southern Drôme, Vaucluse and Gard. The vines, covering an area 60 kilometres wide and up to 80 kilometres long, are basically planted on the plain. The soil is also quite unique, being very arid and covered with round stones to the extent that, especially in Châteauneuf-du-Pape, it hardly looks like soil at all. The grape varieties planted in the southern region are the same as throughout the Rhône Valley (page 54), with the Grenache heavily dominant, and although the 'mix' of grape varieties is wide, the differences in style between the various villages come mostly from the soil and exposition of the vineyards. The vast majority of the wines produced are red, with white wines representing under 1% of the crop. Most of the Côtes du Rhône *génériques* and all the Côtes du Rhône-Villages come from the south. The largest single unit of production is the Caves Coopératives whose name and that of the village will appear on the label.

Châteauneuf-du-Pape AOC

Red and dry white wines from vineyards between Orange and Avignon in the Vaucluse *département*. The name Châteauneuf-du-Pape is world famous, but the wines may still be classified as country wines, possibly because the style of the wine is so allied to the region. The *encépagement* is most original, allowing for 13 varietals: Grenache, Syrah, Mourvèdre, Cinsault, Counoise, Terret Noir, Muscardin, Vaccarèse, Picardan, Picpoul, Clairette, Roussane and Bourboulenc. These last four are white grapes, but they may be used to blend in with the red grapes during fermentation. Minimum alcohol content, very often exceeded, is 12.5° from a maximum yield of 35 hl/ha. The white wines, representing only 2–3% of the total, are proving popular: they have a lovely pale colour, and a floral bouquet that belies the weight of the wine. The reds are generally very good and can be quite exceptional: deep, full-coloured, maturing to a rich mahogany, with a heady concentrated fruit and an aroma of spices (nutmeg), and a warm satisfying finish. Châteauneuf-du-Pape can be drunk young, particularly if the proportion of Grenache is high, but it is at its best at 5 to 15 years after the vintage. Production is about 14 million bottles. Price E.

Côtes du Rhône-Villages AOC

Red, dry white and rosé wines from 17 specific communes in the Vaucluse, Gard and southern Drôme *départements*. Red and rosé wines that may add 'Villages' (or the name of the individual commune) to the simple *appellation* Côtes du Rhône must have a minimum of 12.5° alcohol from a yield of 35 hl/ha as opposed to 50 for the *génériques*. To improve the quality further, the proportion of Grenache is limited to a maximum of 65%, that of Carignan to 10%, and the *cépages nobles* Syrah, Cinsault and Mourvèdre must represent at least 25%. The Villages generally have a deeper colour than the *génériques* with pronounced aromas of blackcurrants or violets, are often rather rough when young, but develop and improve with age. White wines must use the Clairette, Roussanne or Bourboulenc grapes to a minimum of 80%, and must have 12° minimum alcohol. If they are well made, with sufficient acidity, they are delightful as an aperitif or throughout a meal. The rosés, usually from a Grenache–Cinsault blend, are fruity and quite weighty, with enough alcohol to support ageing, but at their best drunk young. The Côtes du Rhône-Villages represents some of the best value for money in France today. About 15 million bottles are produced annually. The 17 communes are listed below alphabetically (Beaumes-de-Venise to Visan). Price C.

Beaumes-de-Venise AOC

Situated south-east of Vacqueyras and Gigondas, this village is better known for its *vin doux naturel*. The red wines are meaty and well made with a good deep colour.

Beaumes-de-Venise VDN

The *vin doux naturel* from Beaumes-de-Venise is made only from the Muscat grape, known as the Muscat de Frontignan. Before fermentation the grapes must have a potential of 15° alcohol and, after the addition of pure alcohol to the must (*mutage*), a total not exceeding 21.5°. A Muscat from Beaumes-de-Venise has a lovely, sunny pale-golden colour, an extraordinarily heady perfume of fresh Muscat grapes with overtones of ripe peaches, and a rich, sweet finish. It should be drunk cold, but not iced, as an aperitif or with desserts as it is too aromatic to go with food. Drink young to enjoy it at its best. Production is almost 1 million bottles, mostly from the Cave Coopérative. Price E.

Cairanne AOC

One of the larger villages, in the centre of the vine-growing area to the east of the Rhône in the Vaucluse *département*, and one of the best. Most of the production comes from the clayey soil and is soft and rounded with a full colour. Vines planted on the stonier soil (*garrigue*) produce a wine incredibly deep in colour, with a rich, spicy bouquet, masses of fruit with a tannic finish that means it should be kept. Most of the wine comes from the Cave Coopérative, which also makes a little white, to be drunk young, a full rosé and even some light *primeur* red. A fine wine from Cairanne is at its best at 2 years after the vintage and can last 10.

Chusclan AOC

Chusclan is situated between Pont-Saint-Esprit and Laudun, to the west of the Rhône in the Gard *département*. Once more famous for its rosé (it shares the same soil as Tavel), the majority of the wine is now red, fruity and attractive, and can be drunk young. The rosé, from the Grenache and the Cinsault, is extremely well made and is at its best the year after the vintage.

Laudun AOC

Situated midway between Chusclan and Lirac, Laudun makes the best white wines of the Côtes du Rhône-Villages. It is pale in colour, with a flowery bouquet from the Clairette grape and, for the southern Rhône, very good acidity. The rosés are good, but not as fine as at Chusclan, and the reds have a good deep colour and a certain spiciness.

Rasteau AOC

An important village, 20 kilometres north and east of Orange, to the east of Cairanne. The soil is the stony *garrigue* from which come the best wines of Cairanne. The most famous wine here is the Rasteau VDN, but it represents under a third of the production of table wine. The red Rasteau is a big wine, very like Cairanne; the whites and rosés are quite pleasant, but there are better wines elsewhere. The reds should be kept for a year or two.

Rasteau VDN

Rasteau VDN is a fortified wine made from the Grenache alone. Only the ripest grapes are used, as they have the maximum degree of natural alcohol. Fermentation is stopped after 3 or 4 days by the addition of pure alcohol, distilled from wine, bringing the total to 21.5°, while retaining the sweetness of the unfermented must. Rasteau VDN may either be 'white' (a deep gold) or 'red' (more tawny), caused by leaving the skins to ferment with the must for a few days. If it is aged in cask for several years, it takes on a flavour known as Rancio, one of the finest VDNs in France and very rare. Perfect as an aperitif, a digestif, or poured into a melon. Price E.

Roaix *AOC*

The village of Roaix lies to the east of Rasteau, near the Ouvèze tributary of the Rhône. The wine, which is mostly red, has slightly less colour and body than Cairanne or Rasteau, but is of good quality, ready for drinking at 2 to 4 years after the vintage.

Rochegude *AOC*

The wine, all red, from Rochegude, comes from vines planted on the plain about 8 kilometres from the *autoroute* exit at Bollène, bounded by Suze-la-Rousse and Sainte-Cécile-les-Vignes. It has a deep plummy colour and a fruity softness and is very good at 1 to 3 years.

Rousset *AOC*

The most northern of the wine-producing villages, in the Drôme *département*, above Saint-Pantaléon-les-Vignes, with whose wine it is linked by the Cave Coopérative. Production is small and the wines are lighter than those from the Vaucluse *département*, but quite fruity.

Sablet *AOC*

Sablet is situated between Séguret and Gigondas, making mostly wine that lacks the rich weightiness of Gigondas, but has a smoothness that sets it apart from the solid, spicy Cairanne. Well-made wines with firm fruit, but easy to drink.

Saint-Gervais *AOC*

The most westerly of the villages, south of Pont-Saint-Esprit, in the Gard *département*. The wines have more elegance than some from the Vaucluse, with good colour and blackcurrant fruit, but they are generally less good than those from Laudun or Chusclan.

Saint-Maurice-sur-Eygues *AOC*

Situated between the much better-known villages Vinsobres and Visan, to the east of the Rhône in the Vaucluse *département*, the wines from Saint-Maurice-sur-Eygues, mostly red, are of good average quality.

Saint-Pantaléon-les-Vignes *AOC*

The second most northern of the wine-producing communes, next to Rousset. These two village wines are made together in the Cave Coopérative. They are typically fruity and can be drunk quite young.

Séguret AOC

Next door to Roaix, with whom it shares a Cave Coopérative, and a kilometre or so north of Sablet. The wines from Séguret have a deep colour, good fruit and are quite robust. They should be drunk at 2 to 4 years.

Vacqueyras AOC

Situated between Gigondas and Beaumes-de-Venise, Vacqueyras has a reputation second to none for excellent Côtes du Rhône-Villages wines. The wines are always very deep in colour with a concentrated spicy bouquet and a powerful velvety impression on the palate. They should be kept 3 to 4 years before drinking and will last 10 years or more. A good Vacqueyras is almost as impressive as a Gigondas or a Châteauneuf-du-Pape and, even if it is the most expensive Villages, offers excellent value for money.

Valréas AOC

Situated to the east of the Rhône, to the north of Visan and the west of Vinsobres, Valréas is one of the 4 villages that make up the 'Enclave des Papes', a Papal enclave of the Vaucluse in the *département* of the Drôme. The size of the vineyard is impressive, totalling over 1,400 hectares. The red wines have a dark velvety colour, are big but not heavy and are generally of very high quality. They are at their best at 3 to 5 years. A little rosé is produced, clean and dry, and pleasant to drink young.

Vinsobres AOC

One of the most eastern of the villages, making a large amount of Côtes du Rhône *génériques*, and a full-bodied, meaty Villages. It is good, but often lacks the depth and character of the villages further south.

Visan AOC

Situated to the north-east of Orange, in the centre of the 'Enclave des Papes', Visan makes a wine full in colour and flavour, but equally full in alcohol. In good years they are well worth waiting for, but otherwise can be a little heavy. Some good white wine is made.

Côtes du Ventoux AOC

Red, dry white and rosé wines from vineyards at the foot of the Mont Ventoux in the Vaucluse *département*. Grape varieties are the same as for the Côtes du Rhône (page 56) and the minimum alcohol content and maximum yield are the same at 11° and 50 hl/ha. The majority of the production of 18 million bottles used to be vinified as a very light red wine, known as a *vin de café*, but the tendency now is to get more colour and body from the fermentation, and to approach the Côtes du Rhône in style. The white wines are hardly seen outside the area, the rosés are pleasant and fruity, but it is the reds that are worth looking for. Very attractive wines, fruity and *gouleyant*, to be drunk at 1 to 3 years. Very good value. Price B–C.

Gigondas AOC

Red and rosé wines from around the village of Gigondas, to the west of Orange in the Vaucluse *département*. Like the Côtes du Rhône-Villages, of which it was a part until it got its *appellation* in 1971, Gigondas must be made from a maximum of 65% Grenache, with a minimum of 25% Syrah, Mourvèdre and Cinsault, the rest being made up with minor grape varieties, now very little planted. Rosés must be from a maximum of 60% Grenache, with a minimum of 15% Cinsault, while the Carignan is forbidden, so they are not too heavy and alcoholic. Minimum alcohol content and yield is 12.5° from 35 hl/ha. The rosés have a subdued pink colour and a heady bouquet and taste. The reds are immeasurably more interesting, with a magnificent deep, almost black, colour, a powerful, briary, spicy bouquet and a rich, tannic taste. They are usually very hard when young, and only start to develop after 3 to 4 years and can last 15 years or more. The concentration of fruit and character makes Gigondas the next best thing to Châteauneuf-du-Pape, sometimes better. Drink with red meats, game and cheese. Production is around 5 million bottles. Quite expensive but worth it. Price E.

Lirac AOC

Red, dry white and rosé wines from vines planted around Lirac and Roquemaure in the Gard *département*, on the other side of the river from Châteauneuf-du-Pape. The reds and rosés come from the principal Rhône grapes: Grenache, Cinsault, Syrah and Mourvèdre, with Grenache representing a minimum of 40%. White wines are made from the Clairette grape to a minimum of 35%, making a pale-coloured white wine with a floral bouquet and good acidity, but produced in very small quantities. The red Lirac is a superior Villages with more elegance and smoothness, while the rosés are almost as fine as from neighbouring Tavel. All these wines must have a minimum of 11.5° alcohol (quite low for this part of the Rhône Valley, which means that the wines often taste lighter and are less tiring), from a yield of 35 hl/ha. Very good with chicken, white or red meats, game and cheese. Good value. Price C.

Tavel *AOC*

Dry rosé wines from just south of Lirac, north-west of Avignon. Tavel rosé may be made from all the accepted Côtes du Rhône grape varieties, but is principally made from the Grenache and tempered by the Cinsault. The minimum alcohol content of 11° is almost always exceeded, as Tavel is a fruity, fleshy wine with a good deal of body. Different *vignerons* make different styles of Tavel: in the past the fashion was for orangy-coloured rosés that had spent some time in wood; today the preference is for pinker, even violet-tinged wines that are kept in tanks and bottled young. Tavel is the most famous rosé in France and is a perfect match for hors d'œuvres, river-fish, poultry and light meats. Drink cold, preferably young. About 5 million bottles are produced a year, all quickly sold. Price C–D.

Côtes du Luberon *VDQS*

Red, dry white and rosé wines far to the east of Avignon, on the right bank of the Durance river in the Vaucluse *département*. The grape varieties, alcoholic content and minimum yield are the same as for the Côtes du Rhône *génériques*, and the wines were at one time sold as Côtes du Rhône. The white wines are light, clean and very attractive when young, the rosés have a pretty colour and go very well with the local cuisine, or with summer meals; the reds are more like the Côtes du Ventoux than Côtes du Rhône in style, with an attractive ruby colour and a soft ripe fruity finish. They are at their best young, not older than 3 years. Production is expanding, especially from the Cave Coopérative, and the wines are very inexpensive. Price A–B.

Vins de Pays

There are so many different local wines produced in the Rhône Valley, particularly in the south, that there does not seem room for more wines or more vineyards. In fact, the vins de pays are either wines grown outside the accepted Rhône Valley *appellation*, but still geographically attached to the Rhône Valley region, or wines produced from grape varieties not usually associated with wines from this area. Prices are generally A.

Vin de Pays de l'Ardèche

Red, dry white and rosé wines which are similar in style to the Vins de Pays des Coteaux de l'Ardèche, which represent over 95% of the total production.

Vin de Pays de la Drôme

Red, dry white and rosé wines from the northern part of the *département* on the east bank of the Rhône. The principal grape for the reds is the Syrah with some Grenache and Cinsault, the wines resembling a light, spicy Crozes-Hermitage or Coteaux du Tricastin. The whites, mainly from the Clairette, are light and aromatic. Production over 2 million bottles.

Vin de Pays du Vaucluse

Red, dry white and rosé wines from vineyards mostly in the south of the *département*. Large production of mostly soft red wines made from the Grenache and Cinsault grapes, in the style of an everyday Côtes du Rhône.

Collines Rhodaniennes

Red, dry white and rosé wines from the northern part of the Rhône Valley, stretching across the *départements* of the Isère, the Loire, the Ardèche and the Drôme. The principal red grapes are the Syrah and Gamay, with a little Pinot Noir permitted in the Loire, and Merlot and Cabernet Franc in the Isère. The whites are from the local Marsanne and Roussanne with Aligoté and Chardonnay and Jacquère admitted, making them a bit crisper than is usual for a white from the Rhône Valley.

Comté de Grignan

Red, dry white and rosé wines from the southern part of the Drôme *département* to the east of the Rhône. The usual Rhône grape varieties are planted, with some Pinot Noir and Gamay admitted for the reds and rosés, and some Chardonnay for the whites. Most of the production is red, resembling a much lighter Côtes du Rhône from the 'Enclave des Papes' in the Vaucluse *département*.

Coteaux de Baronnies

Red, dry white and rosé wines from the extreme south-east of the Drôme *département*. Principal red grapes planted are Cinsault, Grenache, Gamay, Syrah and Pinot Noir, making attractive, fruity wines from relatively high-altitude vineyards. The whites are from the usual Rhône varietals, plus Aligoté and Chardonnay. The Vins de Pays des Coteaux de Baronnies must have a higher alcohol content than most other vins de pays, 10.5° for the whites, 11° for the reds, which makes them a little more serious and full-bodied in style.

Coteaux de l'Ardèche

Red, dry white and rosé wines from a large wine-growing area south of Privas, covering the southern part of the Ardèche *département* down to the edge of the Gard. Apart from the local grapes, Syrah, Grenache and Cinsault, the principal red grapes are Cabernet Sauvignon, Gamay, Pinot Noir and Merlot. Of these, the Syrah, Cabernet Sauvignon and Gamay are very successful as single grape varieties, and offer some of the best-value wines in France. The whites, made with a little Chardonnay, Aligoté, Sauvignon and Ugni Blanc as well as the local grapes, are well made, light and refreshing.

Principauté d'Orange

Reds and rosés from the communes of Bollène, Orange, Vaison-la-Romaine and Valréas in the Vaucluse *département*. The principal Côtes du Rhône grape varieties are used, and the wines resemble lighter versions of *appellation contrôlée* wines from this area.

Provence, the Midi, Corsica

This vast area extends in an almost unbroken sea of vineyards along the full length of the Mediterranean coast of France. In recent years it has been referred to as the 'California of France', and there are indeed certain similarities. The region is incrediby large and varied but, thought of as a whole, the sun is omnipresent, and the rules of *appellation* are perhaps less strict than in other parts of France. Perhaps because of this, but to a greater extent because of the low quality of the wines in general and the unprofitability of wine-growing in the South, the Provence–Languedoc region has become the centre for modern and experimental wine-making and innovative changes in the accepted types of grapes that may be planted. The emergence of the Midi as a potential producer of good wine is the most exciting factor in the current French wine scene.

The vineyards of Provence, Languedoc and Roussillon are some of the oldest in France, having been planted by the Romans. Their wines were well known and of such good quality that they rivalled those of Rome. Two thousand years later, the Midi was best known for *gros rouge*

and over-alcoholic rosés, which only rivalled each other in unpleasantness. Since the 1960s, however, there have been many changes, and much investment, and this dedication to quality rather than quantity is having its effect.

From east to west, the vineyards of the south of France are split into five major regions: Côtes de Provence and Coteaux d'Aix-en-Provence in the Var and Bouches-du-Rhône *départements*; Costières du Gard from the Gard; Coteaux du Languedoc from the Hérault; Corbières and Minervois from the Aude; and Côtes-du-Roussillon from the Pyrénées-Orientales. These are wines of all colours and strengths made from a myriad of grape varieties, the dominant one being the Carignan. In addition to the immense quantity of AOCs, VDQSs and vins de pays, two of the best VDNs in France come from this area – Muscat de Frontignan and Banyuls. Neither must the wines of Corsica, legally a part of France, be forgotten.

Throughout this region, *cépages nobles* – Cabernet Sauvignon and Merlot from Bordeaux, Sauvignon from the Loire, Chardonnay from Burgundy, Syrah from the Rhône – are being planted with great success. The styles, even the names, of the wines are constantly changing. For most wine-drinkers, the future for French country wines lies along the Mediterranean coastline.

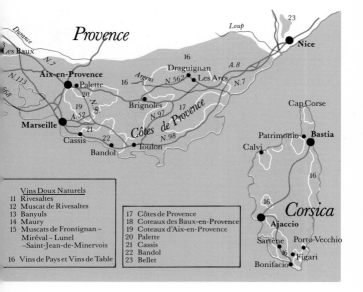

Provence and Coteaux d'Aix-en-Provence

Provence is one of the oldest wine-growing regions in France, with the vines being planted over 2,500 years ago. Best known perhaps for its rosé, it produces some excellent reds and some very attractive dry whites.

Bandol AOC

Red, dry white and rosé wines from terraced vineyards between Toulon and la Ciotat in the Var *département*. Until Côtes de Provence received *appellation* status in 1977, Bandol was one of only four *appellations contrôlées* in Provence, including Cassis, Palette and the very rare Bellet from above Nice. The red wine is without doubt the best wine in Provence, able to rival the finer wines from the Côtes du Rhône. It is made from a minimum of 50% Mourvèdre, which gives the wine a deep, velvety colour and great structure and ageing potential, the rest being Grenache and Cinsault. It must stay 18 months in cask (generally large *foudres*) before bottling, and needs as long again to start to show its quality. A Bandol from a good domaine can last 20 years. Rosés, from the same grapes as the red, but with more Grenache, are salmon-pink with a hint of orange from the obligatory 8 months in wood. They are elegant, consistent wines that go superbly with a Provençal meal. The small production of white, about 150,000 bottles, from the Clairette and the Ugni Blanc, with Bourboulenc and Sauvignon admitted, is generally drunk on the spot. About 3 million bottles are produced. Price C–D–E.

Cassis AOC

Red, dry white and rosé wines from around the port of Cassis, in the Bouches-du-Rhône. This small *appellation*, with only 150 hectares under vines, is known particularly for its white wine. Made principally from the Clairette, Ugni Blanc, Marsanne and Sauvignon, with a little Doucillon (Grenache Blanc) and Pascal Blanc, Cassis is dry, but without acidity, should be pale yellow in colour, with even a little saltiness on the palate. It should be drunk young and is perfect with *bouillabaisse* and all Mediterranean fish. The minimum alcohol content of 11° gives it enough body and the low yield for Provence of 40 hl/ha prevents over-production. Reds and rosés, representing half the 700,000 bottles produced annually, are from the typical red varietals: Grenache, Cinsault, Mourvèdre and Carignan. The rosés are light and fresh, the red often a little dull. Much local demand, especially for the white; prices are high for Provence. Price D–E (white).

Côtes de Provence AOC

Red, dry white and rosé wines from vineyards covering 18,000 hectares, principally in the Var *département*. Côtes de Provence wines were granted full *appellation* status in 1977, as a result of an improvement in quality and further improvement to come. The most popular wines are still the rosés, but the real progress has been among the red and white wines. The whites, representing only 10% of the production, are made from the Clairette, Ugni Blanc, Sémillon and the local Vermentino grape, with some Sauvignon used to add acidity. If the grapes are picked before they are too ripe, the wines are pale in colour, with a floral bouquet and a soft, fruity finish. They must be drunk as young as possible, since they soon lose their freshness, although they may keep. Red wines are made from a minimum of 70% of the following grape varieties: Grenache, Cinsault, Mourvèdre and Carignan, of which Carignan must progressively be reduced to a maximum of 40%. Added to these local grapes are the Cabernet Sauvignon from Bordeaux and the Syrah from the Rhône, both of which bring nuances of flavour and depth. The 'old-style' Côtes de Provence red will be a Carignan–Grenache wine, probably sold in one of the fanciful Provençal bottles, and will be full-bodied, warm and fruity. The 'new-style' wine, made by a growing number of *vignerons*, will have a proportion of non-Provençal varietals in its make-up, and will probably be sold in a Bordeaux bottle under the name of a domaine or a château. These are the best wines from Provence. The minimum alcohol content of 11° is easily attained given the amount of the sun in the region, but the maximum yield of 50 hl/ha is seldom exceeded, especially by those growers looking for quality. Rosés are still the mainstay of the production, and are being made fruitier and fresher to be enjoyed young and cold.

There are three main wine-growing areas in Provence, although there are vines almost everywhere: the coastal vineyards from Sainte-Maxime to well past Toulon; the central plains, south of the *autoroute* from Vidauban to Brignoles; and the vineyards north of the *autoroute* on the slopes around les Arcs and Draguignan. The further north the vineyards are planted, the less full-bodied the wines. Côtes de Provence wines are perfect with the Provençal cuisine: *salade niçoise*, fish or meat cooked with herbs over a grill, all sorts of spicy dishes. The whites and rosés should be drunk cold, and the red wines are at their best chilled if drunk on a hot day. While the vintage plays more of a role in Provence than some more northern wine-growers would like one to believe, with few exceptions the wines, even the reds, should be drunk young. Total production is around 90 million bottles. There are some very good wines to be found. Price C.

Palette AOC

Red, dry white and rosé wines from a tiny *appellation* to the south of Aix-en-Provence near the Abbaye du Tholonet in the Bouches-du-Rhône. The wines of Palette are quite different from their neighbours in the Côtes du Rhône and Provence in that even the whites and rosés need ageing to be at their best. This is due more to the unique soil, derived from the geological formation called the *calcaire de Langesse*, than to the grape varieties, which are the same as throughout Provence. The rosés, particularly those from Château Simone, the major, and almost the only, producer, are more pale red than rosé, while the reds are full-bodied and rather woody. The white wine, mainly from the Clairette, is firm, with some of the character of a white Graves. Well under 100,000 bottles is produced, much of it consumed in the better local restaurants. Expensive wines but a rarity. Price E.

Coteaux d'Aix-en-Provence VDQS

Red, dry white and rosé wines from vineyards to the south and east of Aix-en-Provence in the Bouches-du-Rhône *département*, including a little of the Var. The reds and rosés come from the classic Mediterranean grape varieties: Grenache, Cinsault, Mourvèdre, Counoise, Carignan, with the addition of Cabernet Sauvignon, now admitted to a maximum of 60%. This gives the red wines an intense colour and a blackcurranty-cedary bouquet that is unusual in the wines of Provence. The domaine that has made a great success with the Cabernet Sauvignon is Château Vignelaure. Otherwise the reds are fruity and attractive, mid-way in style between Côtes du Rhône and Côtes de Provence, to be drunk relatively young. The rosés are light and pretty, especially the 'Rosé d'une nuit', a very pale rosé that has drawn only a little colour from the skins. Even with the same alcoholic degree (11°) and yield (50 hl/ha) as Provence, the Coteaux d'Aix wines seem lighter. Whites are made from the Grenache Blanc, Sémillon, Ugni Blanc and a growing proportion of Sauvignon. They should be pale yellow, with good fruit and just a hint of the sun, and no real acidity, so must be drunk young. They are very good with hors d'œuvres and fish. Coteaux d'Aix deserves to be an AOC, and as yet the wines do not fetch the price they should. Production is about 14 million bottles, only 5% white. Price B–C–D (Château Vignelaure only).

Coteaux de Pierrevert VDQS

Red, rosé and dry white wines from the *département* of the Alpes-de-Haute-Provence north-east of the Côtes du Luberon, near Manosque. This is one of the highest vineyards in France, producing mostly rosé from the classic Provençal grape varieties Grenache, Cinsault and Carignan, quite pale in colour, fresh and lively. The whites, from the Clairette, Roussanne and Marsanne, are more like the white Côtes du Rhône than the whites from Provence, with an attractive acidity. Not much seen outside the region. Very inexpensive. Price B.

Coteaux des Baux-en-Provence VDQS

Red, dry white and rosé wines from the region of Saint-Rémy-de-Provence,

Fontvieille and les Baux-de-Provence. These wines are very similar to the wines of Coteaux d'Aix, although they are less well known owing to a much smaller production. The production of white wine is insignificant. The red wines are well worth looking out for. Price C–D.

Vins de Pays

The vins de pays from the *départements* of the Bouches-du-Rhône and the Var follow the same trend as elsewhere in France: they are generally wines made from the same grapes as the neighbouring AOCs or VDQSs, but in different proportions and with a lower degree of alcohol, or planted just outside the delimited region; while the recent experimental planting of *cépages nobles* produces wines which do not fit into the *appellation* and which must therefore be sold as vins de pays. In this region there are 4 Vins de Pays Départementaux and 6 Vins de Pays de Zone.

Vin de Pays des Alpes-de-Haute-Provence

Red, dry white and rosé wines from vineyards in the same region as the VDQS Coteaux de Pierrevert. Grenache, Cinsault and Carignan are the principal grapes for the reds and rosés. Very little white is made. Small production of 600,000 bottles of lively, fruity, relatively light wine.

Vin de Pays des Alpes-Maritimes

Red, white and rosé wines from vineyards on the west side of the *département*. Similar to, but lighter than, the Vin de Pays du Var. Very small production.

Vin de Pays des Bouches-du-Rhône

Red, dry white and rosé wines produced throughout the *département*, but concentrated in the south. Production is very large, over 15 million bottles in 1982, with a high proportion of rosé. The main grapes are Grenache, Cinsault and Carignan and the better wines resemble a Côtes de Provence or a Coteaux d'Aix. Whites tend to lack acidity.

Vin de Pays du Var

Red, white and rosé wines from vineyards in the northern part of the *département*. There is a large production of everyday wines, but they are less interesting than the Coteaux Varois. The reds are better than the rosés, and the whites are rather dull.

Argens

Red, dry white and rosé wines from vineyards around La Motte and Draguignan in the west of the Var. The wines are very similar to the Coteaux Varois, perhaps a little lighter owing to the higher elevation of the vineyards.

Coteaux Varois

Red, dry white and rosé wines from vineyards planted across the Var *département*. Les Vins de Pays du Coteaux Varois represent the second largest volume of vins de pays in the Midi (after the Coteaux de Peyriac), with a production of almost 30 million bottles. The grapes are largely the same as for the Côtes de Provence: Grenache, Cinsault, Mourvèdre and a very high proportion of Carignan for the reds and rosés; Ugni Blanc, Clairette, Grenache Blanc and Malvoisie for the whites. The red grapes may also include some Alicante and Aramon, varieties not admitted for the AOC Provence. Parallel to these classic, deep-coloured, rather heavy reds, are the wines made from Cabernet Sauvignon and Syrah, with more personality and intensity of flavour, but less obviously Provence. The white wines tend to lack acidity and should be drunk very young. There has been much improvement, more at the private estate level than at that of the Caves Coopératives, in the wines of the Coteaux Varois, and it is probable that, under certain conditions, they will be awarded VDQS status.

Maures

Red, dry white and rosé wines from a large area including Saint-Raphaël, les Arcs, Saint-Tropez and Hyères. Total production is 10 million bottles, much of it rosé. The same grapes are used as for the AOC Côtes de Provence, with a high proportion of Carignan. The rosés have good fruit, and should be drunk cold. The reds are unpretentious and should be drunk young.

Mont Caume

Red and rosé wines from the Mediterranean coast of the Var, around Bandol. The grape varieties are Grenache, Cinsault, Mourvèdre and Carignan, producing deep-coloured, full-bodied red wines and very good rosés.

Petite Crau

Red, dry white and rosé wines from the region of Saint-Rémy-en-Provence in the north of the Bouches-du-Rhône *département*. The reds and rosés are made from the Grenache, Cinsault, Syrah, Mourvèdre and Carignan, with the addition of Cabernet Sauvignon. Whites are made from the Clairette, Ugni Blanc, Grenache Blanc and Sauvignon. The reds resemble the Coteaux des Baux-en-Provence with a little less body and the rosés are clean, fruity and refreshing. There is very little white produced.

Sables du Golfe du Lion

Red, dry white, *gris* and rosé wines from vines planted on the sand-dunes in the Golfe du Lion, stretching across the *départements* of the Bouches-du-Rhône, the Gard and the Hérault. This is a large area, and one where there is much experimentation with new grape varieties and ultra-modern methods of vinification. Les Salins du Midi, better known under their brand name Listel, and the government-backed SICAREX are in the forefront of these new developments. The principal grape varieties used for the reds, rosés and *gris* are Cabernet Sauvignon, Cabernet Franc, Cinsault, Grenache, Carignan, Syrah and Merlot. The red wines have a good colour and are attractively low in alcohol, generally around 10.5°. The single *cépage* wines are very successful, notably the Cabernet Sauvignon. The rosés are pale and delicious, the *gris* only faintly coloured, and there is even some *gris de gris* made exclusively from the Grenache Gris and Carignan Gris. The white wines are probably some of the best *vins de pays* from the Midi. The principal grapes are the Ugni Blanc, Clairette, Sauvignon, Carignan Blanc and Muscat, with the Rhône Valley varietals allowed up to 30%. The wines are extremely well made to retain the fruit and slight acidity in the grapes with none of the over-ripeness so typical in the Midi. The whites and *gris* may carry the mention *sur lie* (reserved almost exclusively to Muscadet) if they are bottled off their first fermentation lees after only one winter *en cuve*. With the exception of the reds, these wines should be drunk very young.

The Gard Département

The Roman province of the Gard produces wines that have as much in common with the Côtes du Rhône as with the Midi, while being a little lighter than them both. The *appellation* Costières du Gard is particularly good.

Clairette de Bellegarde AOC

Dry white wine from the commune of Bellegarde between Nîmes and Arles. The only grape permitted is the Clairette and the wine must have a minimum of 11.5° alcohol from a yield of 45 hl/ha. The Clairette is a grape variety seen only in the Côtes du Rhône and the south of France, where it makes a wine with a pale golden colour, a lovely floral aroma of honeysuckle and violets, with soft fruit and no acidity. It must be drunk very young, served cold but not iced. For a dry white wine, Clairette de Bellegarde is the opposite in style to the crisp, lemony Loire whites from the Chenin Blanc. Production is quite small, around 240,000 bottles. Price B.

Costières du Gard VDQS

Red, dry white and rosé wines from a vast region of nearly 4,000 hectares from Nîmes almost to Montpellier. The vineyards very much resemble the southern Côtes du Rhône, basically flat, with an arid, sandy soil covered with stones. The red wines are made from the Carignan (to a maximum of 50%, and much less in the better domaines), Cinsault, Mourvèdre, Grenache, Syrah (from the northern Rhône), and the minor grapes Counoise and Terret Noir. The colour is generally an attractive deep red, and the taste has a typically Mediterranean spiciness and fruit, with some of the roundness of the Côtes du Rhône. They should be drunk at 1 to 3 years. The rosés have just the right balance between fruit and alcohol and make lovely quaffing wines to be drunk within the year after the vintage. There is a little white wine made, only 4% of the 20 million bottles produced, from the Clairette, Bourboulenc and Ugni Blanc. If the grapes are picked early, the whites are light and attractive, with a refreshing clean, soft finish. A great deal of Costières du Gard is sold in bulk by the Coopératives for bottling by *négociants*, and is very good value for money while there are more and more domaines bottling their own wine with very satisfactory results. Price A–B.

Vins de Pays

Vin de Pays du Gard

Red, dry white and rosé wines
from vines planted throughout
the Gard *département*. The
principal grapes used for the
reds and rosés are Carignan
(usually up to 50%), Cinsault,
Grenache, Mourvèdre and
Syrah. The secondary grapes
from Provence, the Rhône
and the Languedoc are
permitted to a maximum of
30%, and the *cépages nobles*
from Bordeaux, Cabernet

Sauvignon and Merlot, are
being planted with great
success. If a wine is made
exclusively from one of these,
it will say so on the label. The
white wines are made from the
Clairette, Ugni Blanc,
Bourboulenc and Grenache
Blanc, with some
experimental plantings of
Sauvignon and Chardonnay.
The red wines have a good
colour, a straightforward
fruitiness and a pleasantly
warm finish. They are good
up to 3 years old. The rosés
are some of the best from the
Midi, fruity and not too
heavy, while the whites are
improving as modern methods
of vinification are adopted.
The price for vin de pays in
the Gard is A, representing
good value for money.

Coteaux Cévenols

Red, dry white and rosé wines
from the north of the Gard
département around Saint-
Christol-les-Alès. These wines

have a little less alcohol and a
bit more acidity than those
which come from the coast,
and have perhaps more in
common with the Vins de
Pays de l'Ardèche.

Coteaux de Cèze

Red, dry white and rosé wines
from the north-eastern part of
the Gard *département*, around
Bagnols-sur-Cèze up to the
right bank of the Rhône. From

this area come the Côtes du
Rhône-Villages-Chusclan,
Lirac and Tavel, and the
wines more resemble the
lighter Côtes du Rhône than
the Vins de Pays du Gard
from further south.

Coteaux du Pont-du-Gard

Red, dry white and rosé wines
from the Pont-du-Gard region
west of Avignon and north-
west of Nîmes. Production is
quite large, around 6 million

bottles, of wine mid-way in
style between the lighter Côtes
du Rhône and the Costières
du Gard. The rosés are
particularly successful.

Coteaux du Vidourle

Red, dry white and rosé wines from vines planted in a small region to the west of Nîmes on the way to Montpellier. The wines are typically 'Midi' in style, very much resembling the Costières du Gard *appellation*.

Coteaux Flaviens

Red, dry white and rosé wines from vineyards planted south of Nîmes, running along the Rhône–Sète canal. Mostly red wines, straightforward and fruity.

Côtes du Salavès

Red, dry white and rosé wines from the vineyards lying to the east of Nîmes. The wines, which are mostly red and rosé, are in the same style as the Vins de Pays du Gard. They have a low yield per hectare of 70 hl.

Mont Bouquet

Red, white and rosé wines from the north of the Gard *département*, just south of the Coteaux Cévenols. In style, the wines come somewhere in between the lighter Côtes du Rhône and the Vins de Pays de l'Ardèche.

Sables du Golfe du Lion

See page 77.

Serre de Coiran

Red, dry white and rosé wines from vineyards to the south and east of Nîmes. This is the same country as Costières du Gard and the wines are very similar.

Uzège

Red, dry white and rosé wines from the region of Uzès, due north of Nîmes. They have much in common with the Costières du Gard, but are a little lighter.

Vaunage

Red, dry white and rosé wines from a small region to the north-west of Nîmes. The Vins de Pays de la Vaunage rosés represent the best wines from this region.

Vistrenque

Red, white and rosé wines from vines planted in a small region at the south-east end of the Gard, on the borders of the Bouches-du-Rhône *département*. The wines are light and easy to drink. Production is the smallest of all the Vins de Pays in the Gard *département*.

The Hérault Département

The Hérault is one of the most densely planted wine regions in France, producing a high proportion of the country's *vin de table*. Improved vinification and grape selection are having a positive effect on the wines' quality.

Clairette du Languedoc *AOC*

Dry and semi-sweet white wines exclusively from the Clairette grape grown in 11 specific communes around Aspiran and Cabrières. The Clairette produces a heavier, more alcoholic wine in the rich soil of the Languedoc than at Bellegarde or Die, from a low yield of 35 hl/ha. It is richer in colour, almost golden, with a full aromatic flavour but a dry finish. Much of the Clairette du Languedoc is not sold as table wine, but is used as a base for high-quality French vermouths. If the grapes are picked late, and the wine reaches 14° alcohol, it is aged for three years and, having acquired a heady, almost maderized taste like a light *vin doux naturel*, it is sold as Clairette du Languedoc Rancio. Generally too heavy to go well with food, Clairette du Languedoc is drunk on its own or with appetizers. Very little of it is exported. Price B–C.

Faugères *AOC*

Red and dry white wines from vineyards to the north of Béziers. The white wine is made from the Clairette, but its production is insignificant. The red is made principally from the Carignan grape, with Cinsault and Grenache in increasing proportions. As with all the Coteaux du Languedoc wines, Faugères must have a minimum alcohol content of 11° from a yield of 50 hl/ha. It is a robust, meaty wine, a good example of wines from Languedoc and very popular in the region.
Production is quite large, at 6 million bottles. Price A–B.

Saint-Chinian *AOC*

Red wine only from vines planted on stony slopes above the Mediterranean in the Béziers region. Saint-Chinian is the largest *appellation* of the Languedoc, with a production of 14 million bottles. Great improvements have been made in planting, with the Carignan grape, permitted at up to 50%, giving way to Grenache and Cinsault; the clayey, chalk-based soil gives the wines a certain finesse. They are not too heavy, seldom more than one degree higher than the minimum 11, and should be drunk at 1 to 3 years after the vintage. Saint-Chinian is quite inexpensive, as the total production is so large. Price A–B.

Cabrières *VDQS*

Rosé wines only from vines planted on steep, schistous slopes outside the town of Béziers. They must be made from a maximum of 50% Carignan and a minimum of 45% Cinsault, the rest coming from the Grenache. Minimum alcohol content is 11° from a yield of 50 hl/ha, but the terraced vineyards rarely achieve this quantity. Cabrières rosé is fine and lively, with a subtle floral aroma and a quite full-bodied flavour. It is without doubt the best rosé produced in the Languedoc. Production is about 750,000 bottles. Price A–B.

Coteaux de la Méjanelle *VDQS*

Red wines, with a minute production of dry white, from east of Montpellier. The grape varieties are the Carignan, Cinsault and Grenache, producing a wine that is dark coloured, rich and tannic, one of the few wines from the Languedoc that repays keeping. Price A–B.

Coteaux de Saint-Christol *VDQS*

Red wine from vines grown on chalky-clayey soil in the region of Saint-Christol, near Montpellier. The classic Languedoc grape varieties, Carignan, Cinsault and Grenache, produce here a wine that is light and fruity and should be drunk young. Production is around 800,000 bottles, mostly from the Cave Coopérative. Price A.

Coteaux de Vérargues *VDQS*

Red and rosé wines from hillside vineyards around Lunel, north-east of Montpellier. Of the usual Mediterranean grape varieties, Carignan is permitted up to 50%, but is giving way to more planting of Grenache and Cinsault, while the *cépage ordinaire*, the Aramon, is still admitted up to 15%. The wines, with 11° minimum alcohol from a yield of 50 hl/ha (often exceeded), are classic Coteaux du Languedoc: full, fruity, sunny wines, uncomplicated and easy to drink, with all the qualities and sometimes the faults of *les vins du Midi*. Production is almost 2 million bottles. Price A.

Coteaux du Languedoc *VDQS*

Red and rosé wines from a vast plantation of vines right across the Hérault, even touching the Gard and the Aude. They must be made from at least 80% of the accepted Mediterranean grape varieties – Carignan (to a maximum of 50%), Cinsault, Grenache, Counoise, Mourvèdre, Syrah and Terret Noir – and must have a minimum alcohol content of at least 11°. The red wines have a fine deep colour and are satisfyingly full-bodied without being heavy. They are a little less good than the Costières du Gard. Rosés are pretty to look at and straightforwardly fruity, and go well with the local food. White wines do not have the right to the *appellation*. Within the region, there are 11 communes that have the right to use their own name on the label, while remaining a part of the global Coteaux du Languedoc *appellation*. These are set out below. Constant progress in wine-making is helping to rebuild the reputation of wines from this area, and they remain very inexpensive. Price A–B.

La Clape *VDQS*

Red, dry white and rosé wines from vineyards on the edge of the Corbières *appellation*, between Narbonne and the Mediterranean in the Aude *département*. Reds and rosés may be made entirely from the Carignan grape, but more usually two-thirds Carignan and one-third Grenache, Cinsault and Terret Noir. They are deep-coloured, well-built wines that age well, especially if they are the old-fashioned Carignan style. The chalk-based soil, rare in the Midi, gives the rosés an unexpected lightness and fruit. The whites, from the Clairette, Picpoul and Bourboulenc grapes, come in two styles: the light, flowery soft wines from the Clairette, and the richer, more golden wines from the Bourboulenc (known locally as Malvoisie), a most interesting wine with finesse and character. The minimum alcohol content for all La Clape wines is 11°, from a yield of 50 hl/ha. They have a high reputation locally, and are beginning to be exported. Production is over 3 million bottles, about 15% white. Price B–C.

Montpeyroux *VDQS*

Red and rosé wines from the hills to the north of Béziers. The red, made from the classic Languedoc mix of 50% Carignan and the rest Grenache, Cinsault, Syrah and Mourvèdre, is a surprisingly good, solid, deep-coloured wine with unexpected finesse. The rosés are typically fruity and must be drunk cold. Price A–B.

Picpoul de Pinet *VDQS*

Dry white wine from vines planted back from the coast, between Sète and Béziers. The wine must come from the Picpoul, to a minimum of 70%, associated with the Clairette and Terret Blanc, reaching an alcohol content of 11.5° from the normal yield in the Midi of 50 hl/ha. Picpoul de Pinet is fragrant and fruity, dry but without acidity. It is absolutely perfect on the spot, with the local Bouzigues oysters. Fortunately, the local demand for the million or so bottles is high, as it does not taste as well outside its own region. Price B.

Pic-Saint-Loup *VDQS*

Red, dry white and rosé wines from vineyards to the north-east of Montpellier. Production of white is miniscule, about 3,000 bottles, mostly from the Clairette. The reds and rosés are typical Coteaux du Languedoc in style, but lighter than most, with a freshness that makes them attractive young. Production is around 3 million bottles. Good everyday drinking. Price A.

Quatourze *VDQS*

Red, dry white and rosé wines from the region of Narbonne in the Aude. The production is almost all red, from the accepted Mediterranean grapes Carignan, Cinsault, Grenache, Mourvèdre and Terret Noir, grown on a stony plateau that gives a dark-coloured, rich, powerful wine. Much of this wine was, and still is, used as *vins médecins*, to bolster up rather lighter *cuvées* of other wines. They are much fuller than the minimum alcohol content of 11°, and will age well. Quatourze is a big, old-fashioned wine, good with roast meat or game. Price A–B.

Saint-Drézery *VDQS*

Red wine only from the commune of Saint-Drézery, outside Montpellier. These are typical 'Midi' wines, high in Carignan, deep coloured and fruity, a little better than the Frenchman's everyday table wine. The minimum alcohol content is 11°, as for all the Coteaux du Languedoc, and the yield of 50 hl/ha is almost always exceeded. Small production. Very inexpensive. Price A.

Saint-Georges d'Orques *VDQS*

Red wines only from vineyards which lie to the west of Montpellier. The grapes planted are Carignan to 50%, Cinsault to a minimum of 35%, and Grenache between 10% and 40%. These give the wine a deep colour and a lot of body, the high proportion of Cinsault bringing finesse. These are wines which can improve with age and are very much appreciated in the region. Production totals about 1.3 million bottles. Price A–B.

Saint-Saturnin *VDQS*

Red and rosé wines made from the classic Languedoc grapes of Carignan (usually 50%), Grenache, Cinsault, Mourvèdre, Syrah. Minimum alcohol content is 11°, from the accepted maximum yield of 50 hl/ha. Saint-Saturnin has a fine ruby colour and is solid and generous, a good everyday wine from the Midi. Production is 2 million bottles, mostly from Caves Coopératives. Price A–B.

Vins de Pays

Vin de Pays de L'Hérault

Red, dry white, *gris* and rosé wines from vines planted throughout the *département*. In 1982 the Hérault produced over 200 million bottles of vin de pays, a quantity exceeding even that of the Aude. The range of grape varieties ' allowed is large: for the reds and rosés the most planted grape is the Carignan, which gives a wine with a fine ruby colour and good body. It is rather hard and common when used on its own, and is limited for AOC and VDQS wines to a maximum of 50% of the *encépagement*. The proportion is much higher for vins de pays, as is the yield (80 hl/ha as opposed to 50 hl/ha), but the Carignan on its own is particularly successful if vinified by the *macération carbonique* process. If the grape is used to 100%, it will say so on the label. Other major red grape varieties for reds and rosés are the Grenache for body and colour, Cinsault for finesse, especially in the rosés, and a little Mourvèdre and Syrah, both deep-coloured, but low-yielding grapes. The *cépages nobles* from Bordeaux, Cabernet Sauvignon and Merlot, are being planted more and more, although their presence is still hardly significant in terms of over-all production, and are very useful as a blender grape to add another facet to the 'Midi'

character of the wines from the south, and are particularly interesting on their own. Minor grapes such as the Aramon, Alicante, Terret Noir, Counoise are still in evidence. The white wines, a very small percentage compared to reds and rosés, are made from the Ugni Blanc and Clairette grapes for the most part, with Picpoul, Marsanne, Maccabeo, Bourboulenc, Grenache Blanc and Muscat. The Sauvignon grape is making progress, since it can flourish in a hot climate, while keeping its natural acidity. Some very good white wines are being developed with modern methods of vinification.

There are 28 different Vins de Pays de Zone in the Hérault, some producing over 10 million bottles, like the Vin de Pays des Collines de la Moure, others, such as the Haute Vallée de l'Orb, producing as little as 700,000. The style of wine is generally that of the Coteaux du Languedoc, with a full colour and good fruit, straightforward, everyday wines. However, new grape varieties and modern vinification combined with a realization on behalf of the producers, who are mostly Caves Coopératives, that quality pays, have moved the brand image of these wines up from *gros rouge* to wines that are well worth drinking. The range of wine in the Hérault is so large and in constant flux that it is impossible to assess each Vin de Pays de Zone as one can different *appellations*, so they are listed here alphabetically with the minimum information given for each. Price A.

Ardaillon

Red and rosé wines, first declared Vin de Pays in 1982.

Bénovie

Red and rosé wines produced in the region of the Coteaux du Languedoc *appellation*, from vines planted around Saint-Christol and Saint-Drézery.

Bérange

Small production of red, white and rosé wines from the Lunel region, better known for its VDN Muscat de Lunel.

Bessans

Red, dry white and rosé wines from the commune of Bessans, in the centre of the *département*, not far from the coast.

Cassan

Very small production of red and rosé wines.

Caux

Red, dry white and rosé wines from vines planted throughout the region of Béziers, south-east of the VDQS Cabrières. The production is large and the wines are generally good, with the rosé being the best known.

Cessenon

Red and rosé wines from vines planted in the commune of Cessenon, between the AOCs Faugères and Saint-Chinian. Large total production, mostly red.

Collines de la Moure

Red, dry white and rosé wines from vineyards planted from Montpellier to Frontignan, in the hills just back from the coast. Very large production of everyday wines.

Coteaux d'Enserune

Red, dry white and rosé wines from the region of Béziers. Large production of everyday wines, mostly red.

Coteaux de Fontcaude

Red, dry white and rosé wines from vineyards planted due north of Béziers. A lower than usual yield of 70 hl/ha helps to give these wines some character.

Coteaux de Laurens

Red, dry white and rosé wines from just south of the AOC Faugères. Production is quite large, around 2.5 million bottles and the wine is above average for a vin de pays. Some interesting wines are made by the *macération carbonique* method of vinification.

Coteaux de Libron

Red, dry white and rosé wines from vineyards following the river Libron, to the north of Béziers. Very large production of fairly meaty red wines.

Coteaux de Murviel

Red and rosé wines from vineyards which are planted in the area to the north of Béziers, on the left bank of the river Orb. Quite large annual production.

Coteaux de Peyriac

Red and rosé wines from the Minervois region, mostly in the Aude *département*. Extremely large production of good-quality red wines, which are almost as good as Minervois, but rather lighter in style.

Coteaux du Salagou

Red and rosé wines from the north of the *département* in the region of Saint-Saturnin. The reds are well worth drinking, being deep-coloured and full-bodied.

Côtes de Brian

Red and rosé wines from the north-east of the *département*, including vines planted at Saint-Jean-de-Minervois. Large production, mostly red wines.

Côtes de Céressou

Red, dry white and rosé wines from the region of Cabrières. Small production of good rosés and full-bodied reds.

Côtes de Thau

Red, dry white and rosé wines from the south of the *département*, near the vineyards of Picpoul de Pinet, planted just back from the coast. There is a very large production of full-bodied, everyday wines.

Côtes de Thongue

Red, dry white and rosé wines from vineyards in the middle of the *département*. Production is very large and there has been some interesting planting of Merlot and Cabernet Sauvignon. One of the better vins de pays.

Gorges de l'Hérault

Red, dry white and rosé wines

from well-situated vineyards planted to the west of Montpellier.

Haute Vallée de l'Orb

Small production of red and

rosé wines from vineyards planted in the Orb Valley, north of Béziers.

Littoral Orb-Hérault

Red, dry white and rosé wines from vineyards planted in the west of the *département*. Very

small over-all production, with some pleasant white wine being made principally from the local Terret Gris grape.

Mont Baudile

Red, dry white and rosé wines from vineyards planted throughout the same region as

the VDQS Coteaux du Languedoc Saint-Saturnin. Quite large production of solidly built wines, mostly red and rosé.

Monts de la Grage

Red, dry white and rosé wines from the region of Saint-

Chinian. Very little wine is produced, as the *appellation* Saint-Chinian is preferred when possible.

Pézenas

Red, dry white and rosé wines from vineyards planted in the commune of Pézenas in the

middle of the *département* between Montpellier and Béziers. Quite good wines, especially the whites if made from the Clairette grape.

Sables du Golfe du Lion

See page 77.

Val de Montferrand

Red, dry white and rosé wines from vineyards planted in the eastern corner of the *département*, north of

Montpellier, near Pic-Saint-Loup and Saint-Drézery. Large production of mostly red wines, full-bodied in the same style as the Coteaux du Languedoc.

Vicomté d'Aumelas

Red, dry white and rosé wines from well-placed vineyards

west of the VDQS Cabrières. Quite large production of good wine, with a high proportion of rosé.

The Aude Département

The wines of the Aude are almost exclusively red, full-bodied and deep-coloured, typified by Corbières. Although the production is still largely of everyday wines, there has been much experimentation with new grape varieties alongside the Carignan and Grenache.

Blanquette de Limoux *AOC*

Sparkling white wines from vines planted in the region of Limoux, south of Carcassonne. The name 'Blanquette' comes from the white dust that covers the underside of the leaves of the Mauzac Blanc grape from which the wine is made. The Mauzac must be planted to a minimum of 80%, the balance being made up by the Clairette and Chardonnay. The still wine has a minimum of 9.5° alcohol from a maximum yield of 50 hl/ha, from which not more than 100 litres of juice may be extracted from 150 kilograms of grapes. It is made sparkling by either the *méthode rurale* or the *méthode champenoise*, keeping the distinctive bouquet of the Mauzac, with a soft, fruity flavour and dry finish. Blanquette de Limoux is excellent as an aperitif, or with fish or chicken dishes. The Cave Coopérative is responsible for most of the 6 million bottles sold annually, and the wine is seeing a justified vogue and expansion. Price D.

Fitou *AOC*

Red wine only from coastal vineyards at the edge of the Aude *département*, on the border of the Pyrénées-Orientales. Fitou has the particularity of being made from a minimum of 70% Carignan, at a time when many growers are replacing this grape with the more supple Grenache and Cinsault. While the other 30% may be from these two, with the addition of Mourvèdre and Syrah, the Carignan makes the wines of Fitou with its very deep, dark ruby colour, rough, tannic fruit and powerful, concentrated flavour. Fitou has to spend 18 months in wood before bottling, and is at its best between 4 and 6 years after the vintage, one of the rare wines from the Midi that age well. It is particularly good with *daubes* and game. The total production is large, around 8 million bottles, and is relatively expensive for the Midi as a whole, but the better wines are worth it. Price C–D.

Cabardès *VDQS*

Red and rosé wines (also known under the *appellation* 'Côtes du Cabardès et de l'Orbiel') from vines grown on the southern slopes of the Montagne Noire, to the north of Carcassonne. Principal grapes are the Carignan, Cinsault, Grenache, Mourvèdre and Syrah, with the Carignan allowed to a maximum of only 30%. Also permitted are varieties from the South-West, such as the Cabernet Sauvignon, Cot, Fer and Merlot. As for the wines of Languedoc and Corbières, the minimum alcohol content is 11°, from a yield of 50 hl/ha. The rosés are pleasant, fruity, everyday wines, the reds firm and lively, a little more interesting, particularly if they are drunk on the spot. Both should be drunk young. Production is just over 1 million bottles. Price A – B.

Corbières *VDQS*

Red, dry white and rosé wines from a vast expanse of vineyards planted between the Languedoc and Roussillon regions, to the south-east of Carcassonne. The reds and rosés must come from the classic Mediterranean grape varieties, Carignan, Cinsault, Grenache, Mourvèdre, Terret Noir, Picpoul (a white grape) and Syrah, to a minimum of 90%. Minimum alcohol content is 11° from a yield, often exceeded, but not for the better wines, of 50 hl/ha. Very little rosé is made, for the reds are much better, solid wines, with a deep, rich colour, a concentrated fruit aroma and a big, meaty flavour. At their best, Corbières can rival any wine from the Mediterranean except Bandol and Palette, and many from the South-West. At their worst, they are heavy, common wines not worthy of the *appellation*. For such a vast production, about 75 million bottles, the proportion of good to bad is high. They may be drunk young, one year after the vintage, while the better wines improve for several years. Red Corbières is extremely versatile, and goes well with any meat-based dish, stands up to spicy food and is excellent with cheese. Under 1% of the production is white, made principally from the Clairette and Malvoisie (or Bourboulenc) grapes. They are attractive, light wines, with a fragrant bouquet and dry, fruity finish, very rarely seen outside the region. Corbières can be found at many price levels, and is often an outstanding bargain. Price A – B – C.

Corbières Supérieures *VDQS*

Red and dry white wines from the same region as Corbières, with a higher minimum alcohol content of 12° from a lower yield of 40 hl/ha. To avoid confusion, this *appellation* is reserved for white wines. Most of Corbières blanc is classified as Corbières Supérieures. Price A – B – C.

Côtes de la Malepère *VDQS*

Red and rosé wines from the region of Carcassonne. The Côtes de la Malepère wines were elevated to VDQS status in 1982, quite justified by the quality of the wines from selected low-yielding grape varieties. The reds must come principally from the Merlot, Cot and Cinsault, none of which may represent more than 60% of the total, and from the Cabernet Sauvignon, Cabernet Franc, Grenache and Syrah, these last four limited to 30%. The wines have a good colour and are quite elegant. The rosés come from the Grenache and Cinsault, the classic rosé mix seen in Tavel and Provence, with juice from the other red grapes allowed up to 30%. They are pleasant and fruity, with a certain body. Price A–B.

Minervois *VDQS*

Red and rosé wines from a large vineyard area north-west of Narbonne and north-east of Carcassonne, straddling the *départements* of the Aude and the Hérault. The wine is made principally from the Carignan (usually over 50%), the Grenache and the Cinsault grape varieties, with a minimum alcohol content of 11° from a yield of 50 hl/ha.

The region is surrounded by mountains, and the hot, dry climate ripens the *cépages méridionaux* to produce a wine with deep crimson colour, a spicy, concentrated bouquet and a firm velvety finish. The concentration of fruit makes the wines from Minervois agreeable young, while good examples can age as well as the better wines from Corbières. They go very well with poultry, red meat, game and cheese. The vast proportion of the production of 30 million bottles comes from Caves Coopératives, as is normal in the Midi, and nearly all of it is red. The wine-growers from Minervois are energetic and are struggling to get their wines better known; meanwhile, most of it remains very inexpensive. Price A–B–C.

Vin Noble du Minervois *VDQS*

Sweet white wine, not to be confused with Minervois, made from the Muscat, Malvoisie, Grenache and Maccabeo grapes. The grapes are harvested very late, and their natural concentration brings them easily to the legal minimum of 13°, with some residual sugar left in the wine. Hardly any Vin Noble is now made. Price C.

Vins de Pays

Vin de Pays de l'Aude

Red, dry white and rosé wines produced throughout the *département*. In 1982 over 150 million bottles of vin de pays were produced in the Aude, 60 million under the many Vins de Pays de Zone, and the rest under the label Vin de Pays de l'Aude. The major grape variety for the reds and rosés is the Carignan, followed by the Grenache, Cinsault,

Mourvèdre, Terret Noir, and Alicante from the south, and in second line the Cabernet Sauvignon, Cabernet Franc, Merlot and Cot from the South-West. In style, many of the wines are mid-way between that of the Mídi and that of the South-West, depending on which grapes are planted. White wines, a small part of the total production, are principally made from the Clairette, Ugni Blanc, Bourboulenc, Maccabeo, Carignan Blanc and Grenache Blanc, and to a lesser degree the Muscat à Petits Grains, Mauzac, Roussanne, Picpoul, Baroque and the *cépages nobles* Sauvignon, Sémillon, Chardonnay and Chenin Blanc. As in the neighbouring Hérault and Pyrénées-Orientales, wines from the Aude are undergoing none too soon a process of improvement and change. Much credit can go to two large Paris-based companies: Nicolas and Chantovent. Their far-sighted investment in vineyards and up-to-date equipment and long-term contracts with the Caves Coopératives created a basis for upgrading the French *vin de table* in the eyes of the consumer and the producer. An example of this are the excellent single-varietal wines, with the name of the grape stated on the label. There are 20 Vins de Pays de Zone dominated in volume by the Coteaux de Peyriac. They are listed alphabetically. Price A.

Coteaux Cathares

Red and rosé wines from the south-west corner of the *département* to the north of the Corbières vineyards.

Coteaux de la Cabrerisse

Red and rosé wines from vineyards in the Corbières region. Both 'Midi' and South-West grapes are planted to make solid, deep-coloured wines.

Coteaux de la Cité de Carcassonne

Red, dry white and rosé wines from the south of Carcassonne, touching the northern Corbières vineyards. The Bordelais grapes, especially the Merlot, do well here, producing deep-coloured, soft, fruity wines.

Coteaux de Lézignanais

Red and rosé wines from the region of Lézignan, one of the better vineyards in the *département*. A very small amount of rosé is made from the total production of 3.5 million bottles of meaty, Corbières-style wine.

Coteaux de Miramont

Red and rosé wines from south-east of Carcassonne below Minervois. Large production of straightforward, fruity wines in the Minervois style.

Coteaux de Narbonne

Red and rosé wines from the region of Narbonne, made mostly from the Carignan grape. The wines are good everyday reds, but not very exciting.

Coteaux de Peyriac

Red and rosé wines from a large area in the Minervois region, touching the Hérault. The reds have a fine ruby colour and more character than many other vins de pays. Very large production of nearly 35 million bottles.

Coteaux de Termenès

Red, dry white and rosé wines from well-placed vineyards situated in the centre of the *département*. Very much like Corbières wines in style and, when the law permits, the wines are sold under the Corbières label.

Coteaux du Littoral Audois

Red and rosé wines from vineyards on the western coastal edge of the *département*, in the same region as the AOC wines of Fitou. Mostly red, deep-coloured and quite full-bodied. The yield is low for a vin de pays at 70 hl/ha.

Côtes de Lastours

Red, dry white and rosé wines from the region of Val d'Orbiel and Cabardès. Small production of well-made wines with a leaning to the South-West rather than 'Midi' style.

Côtes de Pérignan

Red, dry white and rosé wines from the same region as the VDQS wines of La Clape. The whites and reds are light and fruity, the rosés rather heady.

Côtes de Prouille

Red, dry white and rosé wines from vineyards planted in the middle of the *département*. Small production.

Cucugnan

Red and rosé wines from the vineyards situated on the borders of the Pyrénées-Orientales *département*. Full-bodied wines with a sunny 'Midi' flavour.

Haute Vallée de l'Aude

Red, dry white and rosé wines from the west of the *département* in the Limoux region. The southern grapes are not permitted, and the reds and rosés are made solely from the Cabernet Sauvignon, Cabernet Franc, Cot and Merlot, with the addition of Cinsault for the rosés. The whites are from the Chenin Blanc, Sémillon, Chardonnay and Terret Gris. The elevation of the vineyards and the grapes planted make these wines very interesting and quite different from the full-bodied rather weighty style of wines from the Carignan and Grenache grapes.

Hautrive en Pays de l'Aude

Red, dry white and rosé wines from a large vineyard area near the coast to the south of Narbonne. All the grapes that are admitted for the Vin de Pays de l'Aude may be planted. Large production, with quality varying according to the grapes planted and the methods of vinification.

Hauts de Badens

Red and rosé wines from the commune of Badens. Light, everyday wines. Small production.

Val de Cesse

Red, dry white and rosé wines from vineyards north of Narbonne on the borders of the Hérault. Large production, 6 million bottles, of mostly red wine of excellent colour and style. One of the better vins de pays in the Aude.

Val de Dagne

Red, dry white and rosé wines from vineyards planted in the middle of the *département*, south-east of Carcassonne. The whites, principally from the Clairette, are clean and fruity, the reds full-bodied and earthy.

Val d'Orbieu

Red, dry white and rosé wines from vineyards situated in the east of the *département*, surrounded by Corbières and Corbières Supérieures. These are some of the best and most typical vins de pays in the Midi, deep-coloured, full of fruit and sun, yet well made and not too heavy. Some of the most innovative private *caves* are to be found in this area. Production is quite large, mostly of red wines.

Vallée de Paradis

Red and rosé wines from vineyards situated near the Pyrénées-Atlantiques border, just up from the Mediterranean coast. The wines, despite their enticing name, resemble a simpler, lighter style of Corbières.

The Pyrénées-Orientales Département

This is the hottest and driest *département* in France, and the wines reflect this in their full colour and big taste. Côtes du Roussillon is the best *appellation*, as good as anything from the Mediterranean coast.

Collioure *AOC*

Red wine only from steeply terraced vineyards planted in the same region as Banyuls, near the Spanish border. Grenache is the dominant grape, to a minimum of 60%, with Mourvèdre, Cinsault and a very little Carignan. Collioure, with its splendid deep velvety colour, is a rich heady wine with great personality. The lighter *cuvées* can be drunk young, still rather rough and tannic, while the more concentrated wines from low-yielding older vines can last 5 to 10 years. Only the more dedicated growers in the Banyuls region continue to make Collioure and the production is less than 250,000 bottles. It is excellent with the local roast lamb. Price C.

Côtes du Roussillon *AOC*

Red, dry white and rosé wines from the old French province of Roussillon spreading from Perpignan to the Pyrenees. These are the most southern vineyards in France, with vines planted both on the hillsides and on the plain. Reds and rosés must come from Carignan to a maximum of 70%, Cinsault, Grenache, Mourvèdre and a few minor varieties. Along with the Coteaux du Languedoc, Corbières and Minervois, Côtes du Roussillon wines are slowly escaping from the reputation of being *le gros rouge qui tâche*. The reds, mostly made by Caves Coopératives, have a deep ruby colour, a soft, spicy bouquet and a firm, plummy finish. A few *cuvées* are vinified by carbonic maceration, allowing the wines to be drunk *en primeur*, but most Côtes du Roussillon is drunk at 1 to 3 years. The rosés have a striking colour and good fruit. Minimum alcohol content is 11.5°, from a yield of 50 hl/ha, but the wines are naturally fuller-bodied, owing to the long sunny days. The whites are made with a single grape variety, the Maccabeo, which makes a pale golden-coloured, soft, fragrant wine with very little acidity. If the grapes are not left to get too ripe, Côtes du Roussillon blanc is attractive and refreshing and must be drunk young. Production of reds and rosés is around 25 million bottles, with 1 million of white. Very good value. Price A–B.

Côtes du Roussillon-Villages AOC

Red wines only from the most favourable parts of the Roussillon region, around the valley of the river Agly. The wines must have an alcohol content of at least 12°, from a yield of 45 hl/ha, and are deeper in colour, more spicy, more concentrated and more velvety. They age beautifully. The best wines come from the communes of Caramany and Latour-de-France, and are much sought after, and travel well. Only a little more in price than Côtes du Roussillon, so 'Villages' on the label is well worth looking for. Price B–C.

Vins de Pays

Vin de Pays des Pyrénées-Orientales

Red, dry white and rosé wines from vineyards throughout the *département*. Total production in 1982 was 55 million bottles, of which 30 million was declared as Vin de Pays des Pyrénées-Orientales, 25 million under the four Vins de Pays de Zone. The reds and rosés are made with a high proportion of Carignan (often over 75%), Cinsault, Grenache and a little Mourvèdre and Syrah. Grape varieties from the South-West may also be planted for the Vin de Pays, but they are less in evidence here than in the Hérault or the Aude *départements*, owing to the extreme heat. The rosés have an orangy-pink colour, are quite high in alcohol and should be drunk when purchased and not kept. The reds are dark-coloured, full-bodied, sometimes rather rough. White wines are made from the Maccabeo grape with Ugni Blanc and Clairette. If the grapes are picked early, with a good acidity and not too much alcohol, the wines can be attractive and refreshing. Production is largely in the hands of the Caves Coopératives, and while there is less experimental planting in the Pyrénées-Orientales than in the other *départements* of the Midi, there have been great improvements in the quality of the wine in the last five years. Price A.

Vin de Pays d'Oc

Red, dry white and rosé wines from vines planted throughout the south of France, but mostly in the *département* of the Pyrénées-Orientales. The basic grape varieties are the Carignan and Grenache, that make the reds and rosés that represent over 90% of the production of about 10 million bottles. Unpretentious table wines and very inexpensive.

Catalan

Red, dry white and rosé wines from vineyards situated to the south and west of Perpignan down to the Pyrenees. The production is very large, around 25 million bottles, of mostly red table wine. The Caves Coopératives are selling more in bottle and less in bulk, which is a sign that their wines are reaching an appreciative clientele.

Coteaux des Fenouillèdes

Red, dry white and rosé wines from the north-west of the *département* on the borders of the Aude. Straightforward, everyday wines, almost all red and rosé.

Côtes Catalanes

Red, dry white and rosé wines from especially well-sited vines including the cantons of Rivesaltes and Latour de France. The best wines are the reds, with a deep, warm colour and a satisfyingly full flavour. Large production.

Val d'Agly

Red, dry white and rosé wines from vines planted in the north of the *département*, in the region of some of the best Côtes du Roussillon vineyards, Caramany and Rasiguères, whose wines they resemble.

Corsica

Vines were first planted in Corsica by the Greeks, and since Corsica is part of France, this makes the Corsican vineyards the oldest in the country. About 28,000 hectares of vineyards, mostly in the coastal regions, produce 30 million bottles of wine of which 60% is vin de pays. The quality has improved greatly in the last few years since the *vignerons* and Caves Coopératives have committed themselves to producing wines with clean fruit and distinctive style, rather than dull, heavy wines for blending purposes. The long sunny days make whites and rosés that are aromatic, full-bodied and quite low in acidity, and at their best young. The reds, always deep in colour, have a warm spiciness that is said to come from the *maquis*. They are enjoyable young, since although full-bodied they are not tannic, and really do improve with age. A small quantity of *vin doux naturel* is made, as good as the similar wines from France. Corsican wine goes marvellously well with the local specialities of *charcuterie*, strong cheeses and lamb.

Vin de Corse AOC

DOMAINE DE PRATAVONE
VIN DE CORSE

APPELLATION VIN DE CORSE CONTROLEE

DOMAINE DE PRATAVONE

Red, dry and semi-sweet
white, rosé wines and VDNs
from vineyards planted in
specific areas throughout the
country. This is the global
appellation, and wines from
more closely defined regions
may use the name of their
region as an *appellation*
alongside that of 'Vin de
Corse'. The reds and rosés
must be made from at least
one-third (in practice more) of
the specifically Corsican
grape varieties: Niellucio and
Sciacarello, to which may be
added the Grenache, these
three being planted to a
minimum of 50%. Other
grapes include Cinsault,
Mourvèdre, Syrah, Carignan
and Vermentino (Malvoisie).
White wines are made from
the Vermentino and up to
25% Ugni Blanc. The
minimum alcohol content for
all wines is 11.5°, from a
maximum yield of 50 hl/ha.
Most of these wines come
from the east coast of Corsica,
and have the typical spiciness
and warm fruit of wines from
a sunny climate. The whites
and rosés are improving,
being bottled earlier to keep
their freshness and fruit and
an appealing pale colour. The
reds in general have a lovely
ruby colour and have much in
common with the wines from
the southern Rhône. They are
more interesting and less
'common' than their
reputation in France suggests.
Total production, including
all the local *appellations* (see
below), is around 12 million
bottles of red and rosé, 1.3
million of white. The
production of *vin doux naturel*,
mainly from the Muscat and
Grenache grapes, is quite
limited. Price B–C; D for the
VDNs.

Vin de Corse Calvi AOC

*Domaine de
Petralba*

appellation
vin de corse calvi
contrôlée

Red, dry and *demi-sec* white
and rosé wines from the region
of Calvi in the north-west of
the island. The Vermentino
(also known as *la Malvoisie de
Corse*) is dominant in the
whites, producing a wine with
a light golden colour and soft,
fruity taste. The reds are
mainly from the Niellucio and
Sciacarello, deep-coloured,
warm and full of fruit. The
whites and rosés should be
drunk as young as possible,
since they lack acidity; the
reds are at their best at 1 to 3
years. They are very good
table wines, especially with the
local cuisine. Price B–C.

Vin de Corse Coteaux d'Ajaccio AOC

Red, dry white and rosé wines from a vast area of production on the lower west coast of Corsica. The Sciacarello dominates in the red wines, the Vermentino in the whites. Over 85% of the production is red, well-balanced, full-bodied wines with good fruit. Yield is limited to 45 hl/ha and, despite the very southern latitude, the elevation and siting of the vineyards prevent the wine from becoming too heavy. The whites are dry and fruity and should be drunk young. In style, these wines resemble those from the Midi or Côtes du Rhône. Price B–C.

Vin de Corse Coteaux du Cap Corse AOC

Red, dry and semi-sweet white, rosé wines and VDNs from the north-eastern tip of the island. Much less wine is produced now than a hundred years ago. The best-known wines are from the Muscat grape, picked late and sometimes laid out on straw mats to dry out the grapes and further concentrate the sugar (called *passerillage* in French), producing a wonderfully heady VDN known as 'Rappu'. The Malvoisie grape, or Vermentino, makes an aromatic, softly dry white wine, which is well worth trying. Very little red and rosé is made. Price B–C–D.

Vin de Corse Figari AOC

Red, dry white and rosé wines from vines planted in a particularly wild and arid part of the country, directly north of Bonifacio. The Niellucio and Sciacarello are the dominant grapes for the reds and rosés, Vermentino for the whites. In general the wines are some of the better ones from Corsica, full-bodied with lots of character. Price B–C.

Vin de Corse Patrimonio AOC

Red, dry and semi-sweet white, rosé wines and VDNs from vineyards to the west of Bastia. The chalky soil is particularly suitable for vines and Patrimonio was the first *appellation contrôlée* in Corsica, created in 1968. The reds and rosés must have at least 60% Niellucio in their *encépagement*, with a minimum alcohol content of 12.5° (the highest in Corsica) from a yield of 45 hl/ha. They are deep-coloured, solid, rich wines, with a fine bouquet and good keeping qualities, not unlike Châteauneuf-du-Pape. The rosés and whites are lighter and more elegant than most Corsican wines, and there is a little delicious dessert wine made as a VDN from the Muscat and Malvoisie. There are many good wines in Corsica, but Patrimonio consistently produces some of the best. Price C–D.

Vin de Corse de Porto-Vecchio AOC

Red, dry white and rosé wines from mostly coastal vineyards at the south-eastern tip of

Corsica. There has been great progress in wine-making here, with the result that the wines have the best of the regional characteristics from the indigenous grape varieties, and less of the faults of heaviness and oxydation. They are spicy and fruity and the whites are particularly good. Much of the production is consumed by the locals and tourists. Price B–C.

Vin de Corse Sartène AOC

Red, dry white and rosé wines from inland vineyards between Ajaccio and Bonifacio. Grape varieties are the same as for all Vins de

Corse, with a high proportion of Niellucio, Sciacarello and a closely related grape called the Montanaccio, only planted in this region. Minimum alcohol content is 11°, from a yield of 45 hl/ha. The same granite-based soil as is found at Ajaccio, Figari and Porto-Vecchio gives the wines an elegance and firmness, while keeping the rich fruitiness of wines from a hot country. Well worth looking out for. Price B–C.

Vins de Pays

Ile de Beauté

Red, white and rosé wines from vineyards planted throughout the island of Corsica. The principal grapes planted for the reds and rosés are the local Nielluccio and Sciacarello, the Grenache, Cinsault, Syrah, Mourvèdre and Carignan from the southern Rhône, and the Cabernet Sauvignon, Cabernet Franc and Merlot from Bordeaux. The style

varies, and while there is some experimentation with the Bordeaux grapes, the majority of wine produced is still typically 'Corsican', with a soft deep colour and spicy bouquet for the reds, and quite full-bodied, aromatic rosés. White wines are basically from the Vermentino with some Ugni Blanc and recently some experimental plantings of Sauvignon and Chardonnay. Very little of the white is exported. Price A.

Vins Doux Naturels

Vins doux naturels are naturally sweet, fortified wines, not to be confused with *vins liquoreux* which are wines naturally sweet from the over-maturity or botrytised condition (*pourriture noble*) of the grapes when harvested. A *vin doux naturel* (VDN) is the result of the fermentation being stopped early by the addition of alcohol, before the must has fermented out all the sugar. This alcohol is a neutral grape brandy of at least 90° and is added to the must when it contains about 7° of natural and the same amount of potential alcohol. (A wine destined to become a VDN must have at least 250 grams per litre of grape sugar, giving a potential alcohol content of 14°.) This operation is called *mutage*. Depending on the stage at which the alcohol is added, and the amount (not less than 6% or more than 10%), the resulting VDN will have a total richness in alcohol plus residual sugar of between 18% and 23% by volume. The usual level is 21.5%, shown on the label as 21.5°. The finest VDNs, and the vast majority, come from Languedoc-Roussillon. The principal grapes are the Grenache and the Muscat, with a little Malvoisie and Maccabeo. VDNs may be white (the Muscats), rosé and red, and the alcohol should give no sense of burning or roughness. VDNs may be sold at 2 or 3 months, while those made from the Grenache become more complex after some ageing in barrels, which may be left in the sun. These wines take on an aged or 'maderized' flavour, known as Rancio, and these are the most sought-after. Wines of 10 or 20 years old are at their peak, and a great Banyuls may be much older. To the English palate, VDNs very much resemble a fine tawny port.

Banyuls VDN

Red and tawny. It must have a minimum of 21.5° total alcohol, with a maximum of 7% unfermented sugar. It may be bottled young, or matured for several years in cask ('Vieux' or 'Rancio'). Price D–E–F.

Banyuls Grand Cru VDN

Red and tawny. Price E–F.

Banyuls Rancio VDN

More tawny than red. Price E.

Côtes d'Agly VDN

Red, white and rosé. Price D.

Grand Roussillon VDN

Red, white, rosé. Price D.

Maury VDN

Mostly red. Price D.

Muscat de Frontignan VDN

White, the finest and best known of the VDN Muscats. The wines are golden in colour, rich, with a concentrated, honeyed, floral aroma. Price D.

Muscat de Lunel AOC

White. Price C–D.

Muscat de Miréval VDN

White. Price C–D.

Muscat de Rivesaltes VDN

White. Price C–D.

Muscat de Saint-Jean-de-Minervois VDN

White. Price C–D.

Rivesaltes VDN

Red, rosé, white. Price C–D.

Bordeaux and the South-West

Bordeaux is enclosed in the *département* of the Gironde. With some 100,000 hectares under vines, producing around 500 million bottles a year, all AOC, Bordeaux is the largest vineyard of fine wines in the world. Historically, Bordeaux has known three periods of expansion: under the Roman occupation, when the vines were planted; in the Middle Ages, when the south-west of France passed to the English crown and a thriving export business developed towards the British Isles; the period of French investment by aristocrats in the late 18th and by bankers and entrepreneurs in the 19th centuries.

It is a vast region whose range of wines is as great among the lesser-known *appellations* as among the Crus Classés.

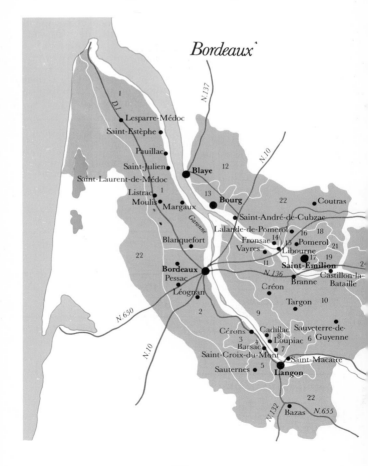

The diversity in character and style is due to the varied soils and climate. The wines can be divided into four categories: red wines from the left bank of the Garonne and the Gironde estuary, embracing the Médoc and the Graves; red wines from the right bank of the Gironde and the Dordogne; red and white wines from the 'Entre-Deux-Mers' region between the Garonne and Dordogne; and the great white wines from Graves and Sauternes.

Bordeaux wines are often sold as 'generics' but are now more usually seen with the name of the property or château more prominently displayed than that of the *appellation*. It is the *appellation* that tells you basically where the wine is from and what it should be like, while the château, domaine or *négociant* represents an individual inter-pretation of the *appellation*.

1	Médoc	14	Fronsac-Canon Fronsac
2	Graves	15	Pomerol
3	Cérons	16	Lalande de Pomerol
4	Barsac	17	Saint-Emilion
5	Sauternes		Saint-Georges-Saint-Emilion
6	Bordeaux Saint-Macaire		Montagne Saint-Emilion
7	Sainte-Croix-du-Mont	18	Lussac Saint-Emilion
8	Loupiac		Puisseguin-Saint-Emilion
9	Premières Côtes de Bordeaux	19	Côtes de Castillon
10	Entre-Deux-Mers	20	Sainte-Foy-Bordeaux
11	Graves de Vayres	21	Bordeaux Côtes de Francs
12	Blayais	22	Bordeaux
13	Bourgeais		

Bergerac

23	Bergerac
24	Montravel
25	Rosette
26	Pécharmant
27	Monbazillac
28	Côtes de Duras
29	Côtes de Saussignac

Generic Appellations

A number of Bordeaux wines are grouped together under the generic *appellation* Bordeaux or Bordeaux Supérieur.

Bordeaux AOC

Red, dry and sweet white, and rosé wines grown in any part of the Bordeaux region, exclusively in the Gironde *département*. Red and rosé wines must be made with the following grape varieties: Cabernet Sauvignon, Cabernet Franc, Merlot, Malbec, Petit Verdot and Carmenère. The minimum alcohol content is 10°, from a maximum basic yield of 50 hl/ha. White wines must be from the Sémillon, Sauvignon and Muscadelle grapes for the most part, with the minor varieties of Merlot Blanc, Colombard, Mauzac, Ondenc and Saint-Emilion (also known as Ugni Blanc) being allowed to a maximum of 30% in principle, but a much lower percentage in practice. Minimum alcohol content is 10.5°, and if the wine has less than 4 grams per litre of residual sugar, it must state *sec* (dry) on the label. Yield is the same as for the reds. This basic, or generic, *appellation* covers not only the everyday wine of Bordeaux, but also those wines which are declassified from higher-quality regional or communal *appellations*, and in addition, wines made in certain *appellations* that are not accepted as part of that particular *appellation*. In the latter case, a white wine made in the Médoc, an *appellation* exclusively for red wine, will have to take the *appellation* Bordeaux (or Bordeaux Supérieur if it is of a higher degree of alcohol), as will a *dry* white wine made in Barsac or Sauternes, where the *appellation* is purely for sweet wines. Generic red Bordeaux is usually of good quality and should be drunk 1 to 4 years after the vintage. Great progress has been made in the vinification of white Bordeaux, of which the dry, crisply fruity whites are deservedly popular, very good value and should be drunk young. The smaller amount of sweet white is pleasant and should be served very cold, as should the very small production of Bordeaux rosé. Price B.

Bordeaux Clairet AOC

Dry rosé wines from red grapes, with more colour than a Bordeaux rosé. The English word 'Claret' is said to have found its origin in this style of wine, which was once the way all wines of Bordeaux were made. Today, it is often more like a very light red wine. Many château owners of red Crus Classés make a Clairet for their home consumption, and it is a speciality of the village of Quinsac in the Premières-Côtes-de-Bordeaux. Serve cold but not iced. Worth looking out for. Price B–C.

Bordeaux Mousseux *AOC*

White sparkling wine from the accepted Bordeaux grape varieties, made sparkling by the *méthode champenoise*. They may be dry or *demi-sec*, determined by the amount of *liqueur d'expédition* that is added after *dégorgement*, and are quite pleasant to drink as an inexpensive alternative to Champagne, or in a Kir Royal. Price C–D.

Bordeaux Rosé *AOC*

Dry rosé wines made from the red grape varieties permitted for generic Bordeaux, with a minimum of 11° alcohol from a yield of 50 hl/ha. The *appellation* Bordeaux Supérieur Rosé may be used if the yield is not more than 40 hl/ha. Very pleasant, particularly if the must is cool-fermented to preserve the freshness of the fruit. Drink very young. Good value and goes with all types of food. Price B.

Bordeaux Supérieur *AOC*

Red, dry and sweet white, and rosé wines of much the same type as the generic 'Bordeaux *simple*', except that the minimum alcohol content must be higher: 10.5° for the reds and rosés, 11° for the whites; the basic maximum yield comes down from 50 hl/ha to 40 hl/ha; and only the *cépages nobles* may be used. They are therefore fuller wines with more character and intensity of flavour. Drink as for Bordeaux. Very good value for money. Price B–C.

Bordeaux Supérieur – Côtes de Castillon *AOC*

Red wines made from the Cabernet Sauvignon, Cabernet Franc, Merlot and Malbec, with a predominance of Merlot. The vines are grown on the right bank of the Dordogne, just west of Saint-Emilion. Minimum alcohol content 11°, from a maximum yield of 40 hl/ha. These wines are as good as, sometimes better than, the lesser Saint-Emilion wines, are underrated and represent excellent value. They have a fine colour, generous fruit and some finesse, and may be drunk at 2 to 6 years. Price C.

Bordeaux Supérieur – Côtes de Francs AOC

Red, dry and sweet white wines from an *appellation* touching the 'Satellite-Saint-Emilions' (see page 114), to the north of the Côtes de Castillon. Red wines, of 11° minimum alcohol, are made from the Cabernet Sauvignon, Cabernet Franc, Merlot and Malbec, with the Merlot dominant, and white wines, of 11.5° minimum alcohol, are from the Sémillon and Sauvignon with a little Muscadelle. The production is 90% red, with around 900,000 bottles a year as opposed to 65,000 bottles of Côtes de Castillon, which they resemble in style, but a little more supple and quicker maturing. The dry whites are pleasant, but less interesting than Entre-Deux-Mers, the sweet whites virtually non-existent. Price C.

Bordeaux Supérieur – Haut-Bénauge AOC

Sweet white wine from the middle of the Entre-Deux-Mers region, grown from the Sémillon, Sauvignon and Muscadelle grapes. Minimum alcohol content 11.5°, basic yield 45 hl/ha. Seldom seen, owing to the fall from favour of inexpensive sweet white wine. Most of the *appellation* is vinified dry and sold as Entre-Deux-Mers. Price B–C.

Entre-Deux-Mers, Graves, Sauternais

Red and white wines are made in the 'Entre-Deux-Mers' region, while the world-renowned whites come from Graves and Sauternes.

Barsac AOC

Sweet white wine grown on sandy-gravelly soil to the south of Cérons and to the north of Sauternes on the left bank of the Garonne. Only the classic Bordeaux grapes may be used, and if the wine is vinified dry, it loses the Barsac *appellation* to become Bordeaux or Bordeaux Supérieur.

Grapes are picked late, affected by *pourriture noble*, and must have the same degree of alcohol and yield as Sauternes. Barsac has all the qualities of Sauternes, and may in fact be sold under that *appellation*, but is more usually sold under that of Barsac-Sauternes. It differentiates itself from the rich, luscious Sauternes by being slightly lighter in style, more lemony. The best Barsacs, 1er and 2ème Grands Crus Classés, produce some of the finest sweet white wines in the world, and can hardly be thought of as country wines. Price E–F.

Cadillac *AOC*

Semi-sweet and sweet white wines from the commune of Cadillac on the right bank of the river Garonne in the southern part of the Premières Côtes de Bordeaux region, opposite Cérons and Barsac.

Only the classic white grapes of Bordeaux – Sémillon, Sauvignon and Muscadelle – are used, and the wine is usually sold under the Premières Côtes de Bordeaux-Cadillac label. Drink quite young and serve very cold. Price C.

Cérons *AOC*

Dry and sweet white wine from vines grown on gravelly-sandy soil on the left bank of the Garonne, to the north of Barsac and to the south of Graves. Only the Sémillon, Sauvignon and Muscadelle grapes are allowed and they are harvested when affected by *pourriture noble*, by successive pickings or *tris* through the vines to ensure the maximum

concentration of sugar. Minimum alcohol content is 12.5°, and the yield of 40 hl/ha is never attained except for the dry wines. These are picked early, and must state *sec* on the label. They have a floral bouquet and some finesse and rather resemble the non-Crus Classés Graves. The classic Cérons is less sweet and luscious than a Sauternes, with a fruity-lemony finish and great finesse. Being generally less rich than a Sauternes, Barsac, Loupiac or Sainte-Croix-du-Mont, Cérons may be drunk with fish and white meats, and as an aperitif, or with fruit-based desserts. Serve cold but not iced. Price C – D.

Côtes de Bordeaux Saint-Macaire *AOC*

Semi-sweet or sweet white wine from vines planted on the right bank of the Garonne, across the river from Langon, at the south end of the Entre-

Deux-Mers *appellation*. The grape varieties permitted are the classic *cépages nobles* of Bordeaux white wine-making: Sémillon, Sauvignon and Muscadelle. Minimum alcohol content is 11.5° from a yield of 40 hl/ha, producing fruity, honeyed wines, a little less rich and intense than Sainte-Croix-du-Mont and Loupiac. At their best young, served very cold. Price C.

Entre-Deux-Mers AOC

Dry white wines, grown in the vast triangle formed by the Garonne and the Dordogne rivers. Geographically, this region also comprises the *appellations* of Graves-de-Vayres, Premières Côtes de Bordeaux, Loupiac, Sainte-Croix-du-Mont, Côtes de Bordeaux Saint-Macaire and Sainte-Foy-Bordeaux. While the minor white Bordeaux grapes, such as Colombard, Merlot Blanc, Ondenc and Ugni Blanc, are allowed, in reality only Sauvignon (now becoming dominant), Sémillon and Muscadelle are planted, in an effort to keep up the quality. The soil is clay-limestone, clay-silicon and gravelly, and the wines produced must have a minimum of 10° and a maximum of 13° alcohol, with less than 4 grams per litre of residual sugar. Entre-Deux-Mers is light, fresh and fruity, with a particular *goût de terroir* that makes it the perfect match for shellfish, especially the local oysters from Arcachon. It is also excellent with hors d'œuvres and fish. It should be drunk young. A good part of the Entre-Deux-Mers region has been replanted with red grapes, which make an attractive, soft, fruity Bordeaux or Bordeaux Supérieur. Both the white Entre-Deux-Mers, with an average production of 13 million bottles, and the red are extremely good value. Price B–C.

Graves AOC

Red, dry white and *demi-sec* white wine from where the Médoc ends, at La Jalle de Blanquefort north of Bordeaux, to south of Langon, an area 60 kilometres long and about 12 kilometres wide. The region takes its name from the soil, whose sandy base with a little clay, full of pebbles and stones, is perfect for the vine. The grapes used are Cabernet Sauvignon, Cabernet Franc, Merlot and a very little Petit Verdot for the red wines, Sémillon, Sauvignon and Muscadelle for the whites. The *appellation* Graves is one of the major regional *appellations* in Bordeaux, along with the Médoc, Saint-Emilion, Pomerol, and Sauternes. It is the only one of these to produce both red and white wines under the same *appellation*. The finest wines come from the northern part, around Pessac and Leognan, where all the Crus Classés are situated. The red classed growths combine elegance and finesse with intensity of flavour, while the white wines are the finest dry white wines of Bordeaux, with the added quality of ageing magnificently. The Crus Classés are, however, expensive, and do not come into the category of country wines. From the middle of the *appellation* come the less complex but excellent Graves red and white, with a minimum alcohol content of 10° (red) and 11° (white) from a maximum yield of 40 hl/ha. The reds have a strikingly attractive fruit, a rose-like bouquet and a fine, smooth finish. They are at their best at 4 to 8 years, but for some wines, modern vinification techniques and absence of wood-ageing make them very drinkable only a year after the vintage. The whites are harmonious, with a floral bouquet and a distinctive, firm finish, with more character and length that Entre-Deux-Mers. They are perfect with shellfish, excellent with hors d'œuvres, fish and white meats. Drink cold but not iced. Good value. Price C–D; F for the Crus Classés.

Graves Supérieures AOC

Dry, *demi-sec* and sweet white wines from the Graves region, with a minimum alcohol content of 12°. Most producers of dry white wine do not bother with this *appellation*, preferring the simple *appellation* Graves and the name of their château.

Most of the Graves Supérieures produced come from the southern part of the *appellation*, between Portets and Langon, and have all the Graves characteristics, together with a certain softness and richness. The current fashion for dry white wine has lost them much of their market. Price C–D.

Graves de Vayres AOC

Red, dry white and *demi-sec* white wines from an enclave in the north of the Entre-Deux-Mers region, on the left bank of the Dordogne. This *appellation* is not to be confused with the Graves *appellation* between Bordeaux and Langon. Here, classic Bordeaux grape varieties produce soft, fruity, Merlot-based reds, and pleasant dry whites, both to be drunk young. Price C.

Loupiac AOC

Sweet white wine from the right bank of the Garonne, opposite Barsac. Loupiac is surrounded by Premières Côtes de Bordeaux vines, but, like Sainte-Croix-du-Mont, it has its own *appellation*. Minimum alcohol content is relatively high (12.5°), and the yield naturally much lower owing to the very late picking of overripe grapes affected by *Botrytis cinerea* or noble rot. If the grapes are picked early and vinified to make a dry wine, the wine loses the Loupiac *appellation*. Loupiac is very like Barsac and Sauternes in style, with a lovely golden colour, honeyed bouquet and luscious sweet fruit. It is delicious young, served very cold as an aperitif or with fruit-based desserts, while the finest wines can last over 20 years. Price D.

Premières Côtes de Bordeaux AOC

Red, dry and sweet white wines from the right bank of the Garonne, along a 60-kilometre stretch from the outskirts of Bordeaux to Saint-Macaire, made from the classic Bordeaux grape varieties. The northern part, nearer Bordeaux, produces red and Clairet wines, the southern part of the vineyard being better known for its semi-sweet and sweet whites, although much replanting of red grapes has been done. Production is limited to 40 hl/ha, minimum alcohol content is 10.5° for the reds (11.5° if the name of the commune is added, e.g. Premières Côtes de Bordeaux-Quinsac), 12° for the whites. The red wines are soft and generous, with a fine ruby colour, a little harsh *en primeur*, but acquiring suppleness and depth with age, up to 6 to 7 years. The sweet whites are late picked in the Sauternes manner, and are now well vinified, rich and perfumed. They are both excellent value. Price B–C.

Sainte-Croix-du-Mont AOC

Sweet white wine from vineyards sloping down to the right bank of the Garonne, just south of Loupiac on the other side of the river from Sauternes. The wine is made from the Sémillon, Sauvignon and Muscadelle grapes, picked late when affected by *pourriture noble*. The minimum alcohol content is 12.5°, and the legal maximum yield of 40 hl/ha is almost never attained. Owing to the decline in popularity of sweet wine, much of the crop is picked early and vinified *en sec* to be sold under the *appellation* Bordeaux. True Sainte-Croix-du-Mont is pale gold in colour when young, deepening to amber with age, honeyed, rich and unctuous, with great finesse. The better wines are fine and long lasting. They may be drunk young, to appreciate the explosive richness of fruit, or kept for up to 25 years. They are painstakingly made wines and are good value. Price D.

Sainte-Foy-Bordeaux AOC

Red, dry white and sweet white wine from the north-eastern extremity of the Gironde *département*, on the left bank of the Dordogne. Even though geographically part of the Entre-Deux-Mers region, the wines are quite different.

They are made from the classic Bordeaux varieties, and must have 10.5° minimum alcohol for the reds, 11° for the whites, from a maximum yield of 45 hl/ha. In the past, the wines were *demi-sec* or sweet, and were known as 'the poor man's Sauternes', but now that the Sauvignon is planted more and more, the wines are mostly dry and pleasantly fruity. The reds have a good deep colour and are full-bodied with an attractive soft fruit that allows them to be drunk young. Price B – C.

Sauternes AOC

Sweet white wine grown on the left bank of the Garonne, south of Barsac and the west of Langon. The Sémillon (heavily dominant), Sauvignon and Muscadelle grapes combine to make the finest sweet white wine in France. The minimum alcohol content of 12.5° is usually surpassed, with many degrees of residual sugar remaining after fermentation. The low yield of 25 hl/ha is rarely attained. Sauternes must be made with grapes already attacked by *pourriture noble*, which flourishes in the micro-climate of humid early mornings and, if they are lucky, hot autumn days. The grapes are picked at the maximum concentration of sugar, the pickers going through the vines several times, picking bunch by bunch, even grape by grape. These incredibly luscious, intense, elegant wines are known mostly through their Grands Crus Classés. Sauternes may be drunk young, but should really be kept to 10, 20, 50 years old. Price E – F.

Wines from the Right Bank

The vineyards on the right banks of the Gironde and the Dordogne produce generally full-bodied red wines.

Blaye or Blayais AOC

Red, dry white and sweet white wines from the right bank of the Gironde estuary. To the basic red grape varieties may be added the Cot, and to the whites the Folle Blanche and Frontignan. Red and white wines have the same minimum alcohol content, 10°, from a yield of 45 hl/ha for the whites, 50 hl/ha for the reds. The quantity of red wine which is produced is tiny, most of it being upgraded to Premières Côtes de Blaye. The white wines, which are predominantly dry, are pleasant and should be drunk very young. Price B – C.

Côtes de Blaye AOC

Dry or sweet white wines, from the same region as the Blayais wine, but with a higher minimum alcohol content of 10.5°. In general the sweet wines have given way to the fruity, dry wines from the Sauvignon and the Sémillon grapes. Good value, but without the floral finesse of the best Entre-Deux-Mers. Price B–C.

Premières Côtes de Blaye AOC

Red, dry, *demi-sec* and sweet white wines grown on the right bank of the Gironde, opposite the Médoc. Same yield as for the Blayais wine, but with 0.5° more alcohol. Only Cabernet Sauvignon, Cabernet Franc, Malbec and Merlot are permitted for the reds, which have a good colour and a straightforward, soft, fruity taste. They are lighter, but have more finesse on the nose than their neighbour the Côtes de Bourg. A great deal of good-value red wine is produced and a very small amount of white, which is usually sweet. Price B–C.

Bourg-Bourgeais AOC

Red, dry, *demi-sec* and sweet white wines from the canton of Bourg-sur-Gironde, south of the Blayais on the right bank of the Gironde opposite the Haut-Médoc. Both red and white wines are made only from the *cépages nobles* of Bordeaux. Over 90% of the production is red, making a deep-coloured, robust, high-quality Bordeaux with good ageing potential. They are excellent at 2 to 6 years, can last even longer, and are much underrated in comparison to the Médocs from across the river. Very good with chicken, red meats and cheese. Price C–D.

Côtes de Bourg AOC

Red and dry white wines from the Bourgeais. This *appellation* is often used as an alternative to that of Bourgeais, except that the white wines must be dry. Price C–D.

Canon Fronsac AOC

Red wines from the Fronsac region, but from the best-situated vineyards. The wines are made from the same grape varieties as those from Fronsac, with the same minimum alcohol content of 11° from a yield of 42 hl/ha. Legally, this *appellation* should be called Côtes Canon Fronsac. They have a very deep colour, are solid, robust, meaty wines, with a velvety intenseness of flavour, a certain spiciness and great finesse. They may be drunk after 4 to 5 years, reach their best at 10 years and can last 20. Canon Fronsacs are said to resemble the wines of Pomerol, or even Burgundy, and have also been referred to as 'classic, old-fashioned claret'. These are marvellous wines with red meats. Excellent value. Price D–E.

Fronsac AOC

Red wines only from vineyards planted on the right bank of the Dordogne, north-east of Libourne. This *appellation* used to be known as Côtes de Fronsac. The wines are made from the Cabernet Sauvignon, Cabernet Franc, Merlot and Malbec grapes, often in the proportion of 50% Cabernets, 50% Merlot, producing solid, robust wines with an excellent deep colour, some depth and great potential. They are at their best at 4 to 10 years, and are greatly appreciated by those who cannot or will not pay for the Crus Classés. A perfect wine for red meats and cheese. Serve *chambré*. Excellent value. Price C–D.

Lalande de Pomerol AOC

Red wines from vines grown to the north of Pomerol on a sandy-gravelly soil. The grapes are Cabernet Sauvignon, Cabernet Franc, Merlot and Malbec, with Merlot dominant, producing a deep-coloured, rich velvety wine, not unlike Pomerol, but with less finesse. Minimum alcohol content 10.5°, yield 40 hl/ha. They are apt to be tough and lacking in charm when young, but age well. Excellent with red meats, game and cheese. Price E.

Lussac Saint-Emilion AOC

Red wines from the slopes north of Saint-Emilion to the west of Pomerol. This and the following four *appellations* are known as the 'Satellite-Saint-Emilions', since they surround the Saint-Emilion *appellation* and their wines are of the same style. The grapes permitted are the same as for Saint-Emilion. Lussac Saint-Emilion is ready to drink young, at 3 to 4 years, and fades after about 8 years. The best are as good as, and the same price as, the Saint-Emilion Grands Crus. Price C–D.

Montagne Saint-Emilion AOC

Red wines from vineyards to the north of Saint-Emilion and to the west of Pomerol. The same rules of *appellation* apply as in Saint-Emilion, whose wines they resemble, often giving better value than the more popular Saint-Emilions. Vines planted on the higher slopes on a chalky-clayey soil give a more robust wine than those planted on the gravelly soil towards Pomerol. Price C–D.

Néac AOC

Red wines from vineyards north of Pomerol, between Lalande de Pomerol and Montagne-Saint-Emilion. The wines are of fine quality, deep in colour, generous, with some of the class of Pomerol and the richness of Saint-Emilion. Virtually everything produced in this area is now declared as Lalande de Pomerol. Price E.

Parsac-Saint-Emilion AOC

Red wines from vineyards to the north of Saint-Emilion. Since 1973, the wines are sold under the *appellation* Montagne Saint-Emilion. Price C–D.

Pomerol AOC

Red wines from the right bank of the Dordogne to the north-west of Libourne. The soil is sandy-gravelly with a little clay and only the *cépages nobles* are planted, with Merlot dominant. Pomerol has a rich, ruby colour, a suave, almost 'animal' bouquet and a long velvety finish. They have become justifiably fashionable and from their price and scarcity are hardly country wines. Price E, mostly F.

Puisseguin-Saint-Emilion AOC

Red wines from the north-east of Saint-Emilion. The same grape varieties are planted on a stony clayey-chalky soil, and produce wines that are full-coloured and robust, very much in the Saint-Emilion style, and keep well. None the less, Puisseguin is generally less fine than either Saint-Georges or Montagne Saint-Emilion. Price C – D.

Saint-Emilion AOC

Red wines from the right bank of the Dordogne, south-west of Pomerol. The regional *appellation* Saint-Emilion is divided into Saint-Emilion 1er Grands Crus Classés (comprising the 12 finest châteaux), Saint-Emilion Grands Crus Classés (some 70 châteaux), Saint-Emilion Grands Crus (whose list of châteaux is fixed each year by official tastings) and Saint-Emilion. Grape varieties are the Cabernet Sauvignon (called Bouchet in the region), Cabernet Franc, Merlot and Malbec. The Merlot is largely dominant, sometimes up to 80%. Saint-Emilion must

have 11° minimum alcohol, 11.5° for the Grands Crus, from a basic maximum yield of 42 hl/ha, which is often exceeded for the lesser wines. Total production is around 24 million bottles a year. Saint-Emilion wines are divided into two styles by the nature of the soil: the 'Graves', sandy-gravelly soil adjacent to Pomerol, and the 'Côtes', undulating vineyards with a clayey-chalky soil. The true Saint-Emilion style is a rich, full-coloured wine, with concentrated fruit, and an apparent sweetness due to a low degree of tannin. They are at their best at 6 to 12 years, but the minor wines may be drunk at 2 to 3 years. The 'Graves' wines have more bouquet, while the 'Côtes' are closer-knit. Saint-Emilion wines are often referred to as 'the Burgundies of Bordeaux', and as such go well with red meats, game and cheese. There are some good values to be had from the minor châteaux. Price D – E (Grands Crus Classés); F (1er Grands Crus Classés).

Saint-Georges-Saint-Emilion AOC

Red wines from vineyards which are planted to the north-east of Saint-Emilion, touching those of Montagne Saint-Emilion. All the vines are planted on the 'Côtes', and produce a more robust wine, with a deep colour, powerful yet elegant, that ages beautifully. These wines are the finest of the Satellite-Saint-Emilions, along with Montagne Saint-Emilion, under which *appellation* they may be sold. Very good value. Price C – D.

Wines from the Médoc

The Médoc region produces red wines with a fine, deep colour and great character.

Haut-Médoc AOC

Red wines from the southern part of the Médoc *appellation*. Permitted grapes are the same as for the Médoc, minimum alcohol content is higher at 10.5°, yield lower at 40 hl/ha. Wines from the Haut-Médoc have more elegance, intensity of flavour and finesse than those from the Médoc. Virtually everything is sold under a château label, and the Crus Classés from the Haut-Médoc cannot be considered as country wines. However, the very many Crus Bourgeois can be, and represent good value for money. Price D – E.

Médoc AOC

Red wine from a stretch of vineyards 80 kilometres long and 10 kilometres wide, running along the left bank of the Gironde, from Blanquefort to the tip of the estuary. The Médoc is divided into two regions: the Haut-Médoc, from Blanquefort to Saint-Seurin-de-Cadourne, which also includes the *appellations communales* of Listrac, Moulis, Margaux, Saint-Julien, Pauillac and Saint-Estèphe, and the Médoc, from Saint-Seurin northwards. The grapes permitted are the classic Bordeaux varieties: Cabernet Sauvignon (usually the single dominant grape), Cabernet Franc, Merlot, with a small amount of Malbec and Petit Verdot. It is the Médoc soil, a pebbly-gravelly top-soil on a clay, limestone and chalk base, that allows the vine to thrive and gives the wine its particular character. Vines planted on the alluvial soil close to the river only have the right to the *appellation* Bordeaux or Bordeaux

Supérieur, as do the few dry, white wines produced in the red-wine-producing Médoc. Minimum alcohol content is 10°, maximum yield 45 hl/ha. Wines from the Médoc have a fine, deep colour from the Cabernet Sauvignon, a complex bouquet reminiscent of blackcurrants and spice and an intense fruit on the palate, austere when young, but always pure and harmonious.

They are at their best at 6 to 12 years, but wines from fine châteaux in good years will last longer. The minor wines of the Médoc, either sold as generics, or under a château label, represent excellent value for money. They are perfect with poultry, red meats, especially lamb, and cheese. Production is around 12 million bottles a year. Price D–E.

Listrac *AOC*

Red wines from the inland part of the Haut-Médoc, to the east of Margaux. With the same *appellation* rules, Listrac is a little tougher at first than other Haut-Médocs, but has the same deep colour, and opens up well after four or five years. It is perhaps the least prestigious of the *appellations communales* and is usually good value. Price D–E.

Margaux *AOC*

Red wine from the most southern of the *appellations*

communales in the Haut-Médoc, comprising the communes of Margaux, Cantenac, Soussans, Labarde and Arsac. The Cabernet and Merlot grapes combine to make a wine of extreme finesse, intense in flavour but never heavy. The reputation of its wines generally justifies the high price of the Grands Crus Classés, while the less pricy Crus Bourgeois can be very fine. Price E–F.

Moulis *AOC*

Red wines from the Haut-Médoc, just to the south of Listrac. A very high level of chalk in the soil gives Moulis its particular suave character, quicker developing than other Haut-Médocs, with great finesse. The wine is often referred to as Moulis en Médoc. The lesser known châteaux are very good value. Price D–E.

Pauillac AOC

Red wine from the commune of Pauillac, situated between Saint-Julien to the south and Saint-Estèphe to the north. Wines from Pauillac are generally recognized to be the most classic in the Médoc: they have a deep, intense colour, a bouquet of great distinction and are both full-bodied and elegant on the palate. Pauillacs are the longest-lived red wines from Bordeaux and, when young, their slightly hard flavour is described by the English as 'lead pencil' and by the French as *un goût de capsule*. The commune harbours the largest number of Grands Crus Classés. Price E–F.

Saint-Estèphe AOC

Red wine from the largest and most northerly of the *appellations communales* of the Haut-Médoc. Saint-Estèphes are deep-coloured, solid, meaty wines, which age wonderfully. With the exception of the Grands Crus Classés and several excellent Crus Bourgeois (particularly around the village of Pez), Saint-Estèphe has less finesse than Margaux, Saint-Julien or Pauillac, but is very satisfying. There is an excellent Cave Coopérative. Price E–F.

Saint-Julien AOC

Red wine from the commune of Saint-Julien-Beychevelle, Cussac and Saint-Laurent, almost in the centre of the Médoc. Permitted grapes, as for all the *appellations communales* of the Haut-Médoc, are the same as for the Médoc, with minimum alcohol 10.5° from a yield of 40 hl/ha. Wines from Saint-Julien are very fine, combining the finesse of Margaux to the south and the body of Pauillac to the north. They are the perfect example of Claret, and the Saint-Julien Grands Crus Classés are much sought after. Price E–F.

The Wines of the South-West

The South-West covers a large range of wines from the *départements* of Aveyron, Cantal, Dordogne, Gers, Haute-Garonne, Landes, Lot, Lot-et-Garonne, Pyrénées-Atlantiques, Tarn and Tarn-et-Garonne. Despite the range of soils, climates and grape varieties, the wines do seem to have a recognizable style. The reds, the majority of the production, have a rich, dark colour and a certain rusticity, rather hard when young but ageing well. There are some excellent rosés. The dry whites are little known, while the sweet whites offer the famous Jurançon and Monbazillac. Much of the white is made sparkling by the *méthode champenoise* or *méthode rurale*. The wines of the South-West are seeing a deserved revival in popularity.

Béarn *AOC*

Red, rosé and dry white wines, principally from the *département* of the Pyrénées-Atlantiques. The province of Béarn also covers the wines of Irouléguy, Jurançon, Pacherenc du Vic Bihl and Madiran. Reds and rosés must be from the local grape, the Tannat, to a maximum of 60%, and other indigenous varietals such as Manseng Noir, Fer, Pinenc, Courbu Noir, along with Cabernet Sauvignon and Cabernet Franc from Bordeaux. They are fruity, agreeable and quite light, perfect with the Basque cuisine. Most is produced by Caves Coopératives and much is drunk by locals and tourists at 1 to 2 years old, although the red may be kept longer. The white wine, under 10% of the *appellation*, is from a mixture of local grapes: Petit-Manseng, Gros-Manseng, Courbu, Lauzat, Baroque, with the addition of Sémillon and Sauvignon. They are light and dry, but lack a little character and acidity and do not travel well. All Béarn wines must have 10.5° minimum alcohol from a basic maximum yield of 50 hl/ha. Average production is 750,000 bottles. Price C.

Bergerac *AOC*

Red and rosé wines from the Bergerac region in the *département* of the Dordogne. Already well known in the late Middle Ages, they are just now recovering their reputation. Grapes permitted are the Bordeaux varietals: Cabernet Sauvignon, Cabernet Franc, Merlot and Malbec, as well as the Fer. The wines must reach a minimum alcohol content of 10°, from a yield of 50 hl/ha. The Dordogne divides the wines into two styles: those from the right bank are softer and have more finesse, those from the left bank are deeper in colour, fuller-bodied and more tannic. Bergerac resembles the red Entre-Deux-Mers with a lighter, more pronounced fruit, and they should be drunk relatively young, at 1 to 4 years. The rosés have a pretty pink colour, are refreshing and vivacious, but are less interesting than the reds. Production is around 15 million bottles. Price B–C.

Bergerac sec AOC

Dry white wine from the Bergerac region. Grape varieties are the Sémillon, Sauvignon and Muscadelle, with a little Ondenc and Chenin Blanc, producing a wine with a minimum alcohol content of 11°, from a yield of 50 hl/ha. In the past, white Bergerac used to be sweet, but this is being reversed with the increased planting of Sauvignon. The wines are crisp and dry with a pleasant fruit, the finest from the *cru* Panisseau. Drink very young, with *charcuterie*, fish and poultry. Price B–C.

Cahors AOC

Red wine from vineyards planted on both banks of the Lot river, in the Quercy *département*. The vineyards of Cahors are some of the oldest in France, being already well known under the Roman occupation. The *encépagement* is most original: a minimum of 70% Malbec (known locally as the Auxerrois, and in the Loire Valley as the Cot), a maximum of 20% Merlot and Tannat, with 10% Jurançon Noir. The wine produced is very deep in colour, a dark crimson, almost black when very young, is solid, meaty, pleasantly rough at first, smoothing out after 3 years into a wine of great harmony and distinction. The relative lightness in alcohol, 10.5° minimum with a maximum of 13°, from a yield of 50 hl/ha, belies the body and flavour. The expression 'Vieux Cahors' is for wines aged for 3 years in wood. Cahors is perfect with the local Quercyois cuisine, fabulous with *confit de canard* and is a rival to Madiran to accompany a *cassoulet*. There has been much replanting in the region, and while most of the *appellation* produces good-quality wines, a few are distressingly light. Production is slightly over 10 million bottles. Price C–D.

Côtes de Bergerac AOC

Red wines from the Bergerac region, made with the same grapes as Bergerac, but with a minimum alcohol content of 11°. The difference between Bergerac and Côtes de Bergerac is similar to that between Bordeaux and Bordeaux Supérieur: the wines have more depth and personality, and are well worth the little extra money. Just over 2 million bottles are produced. Price B–C.

Côtes de Bergerac – Côtes de Saussignac AOC

White wine, usually dry, from 5 communes around Saussignac in the Bergerac region. The wines must reach 12.5° alcohol to have the right to the *appellation* Côtes de Saussignac, which makes them a bigger, more mouth-filling wine than Bergerac sec. Good with *charcuterie*, fish and white meats. Around 300,000 bottles are produced. Price C.

Côtes de Bergerac Moelleux AOC

Sweet white wine from the Bergerac region, made from the Sémillon, Sauvignon and Muscadelle grapes. The wines should have between 12° and 15° alcohol and residual sugar combined. These delightful, soft, fruity wines are still popular in France and Northern Europe, and are relatively inexpensive. Price C.

Côtes de Buzet AOC

Red, dry white and rosé wines from the region between Agen and Casteljaloux on the left bank of the Garonne, in the Lot-et-Garonne *département*. The red wines are made from the Cabernet Sauvignon, Cabernet Franc and Merlot, with a very little Malbec, essentially the *encépagement Bordelaise*. The majority of the wine is vinified by the Cave Coopérative at Buzet-sur-Baïse, and has an excellent colour, with all the elegance of the Cabernets and the soft fruit of the Merlot. They are excellent dinner wines, to be drunk between 3 and 8 years. The Cuvée Napoléon is the prestige wine, aged in new oak casks and has the quality of a good Médoc. White wines, only 2–3% of the *appellation*, are made from the Sémillon, Sauvignon and Muscadelle and resemble the everyday dry, white Bordeaux with a little more body. The production of rosé is insignificant. All wines have a minimum of 10° alcohol from a yield of 40 hl/ha. The vineyards of Côtes de Buzet are in full expansion, as the wine is justifiably popular. Price C–D.

Côtes de Duras AOC

Red, dry white and sweet white wines from the north of the Lot-et-Garonne *département*, between the vineyards of Entre-Deux-Mers and Bergerac. The red wines are from the Cabernet Sauvignon, Cabernet Franc, Merlot and Malbec, with a minimum alcohol content of 10° from a yield of 50 hl/ha. They are pleasant and fruity, easy to drink young, like a simple Bordeaux. The white wines, whose production at around 4.5 million bottles is almost double that of the red, are from Sémillon, Sauvignon and Muscadelle, with the local grapes Mauzac and Ondenc, and up to 25% Ugni Blanc. The sweet white used to dominate, but now the crisp dry Sauvignon-based whites are more popular. Both, with a minimum degree of 10.5°, have a distinctive bouquet and a clean, fruity finish. They are not yet well known and are excellent value. Price B.

Côtes de Montravel – Haut Montravel AOC

Sweet white wine from the region of Montravel. These two *appellations* are for wines from the hill-side vineyards planted in certain specific communes. The more simple Montravel comes from vineyards on the plain, and represents 85% of the global Montravel *appellation*. Only the Sémillon, Sauvignon and Muscadelle grapes are permitted, and the wines must have a minimum of 12° alcohol, a maximum of 15° plus residual sugar. They resemble the better Premières Côtes de Bordeaux. Price C.

Côtes du Frontonnais AOC

Red and rosé wines from a small vineyard area north of Toulouse in the *départements* of the Haute-Garonne and Tarn-et-Garonne. The grapes are up to 70% the local Negrette, the balance being made up with Cabernet Sauvignon, Cabernet Franc, Malbec, Cinsault, Syrah, Mauzac and, in ever-growing proportions, Gamay. Minimum alcohol content is 10.5°, maximum 13°, from a yield of 50 hl/ha. The wines have a very good colour, are fruity and well structured. They may be drunk young, but can last 3 to 4 years. Some of the best wines come from the commune of Villaudric, whose name may be added to Côtes du Frontonnais on the label. Quite inexpensive. Price B.

Gaillac AOC

Red, rosé, dry and *demi-sec* whites and sparkling wines from the Tarn *département*, around the towns of Albi and Castres. The Gaillac vineyards are some of the oldest in France, dating from the pre-Christian era. Its wines are quite diverse: fruity, aromatic reds and rosés, clean dry whites, sweet whites, and wines fully sparkling, slightly sparkling or simply *perlé*. The Tarn river divides the region into two styles of wine: those from the chalky slopes on the right bank tend to be richer and more aromatic; those from the granity soil on the left bank are crisper and more lively. The white wines, representing rather more than half the total production of 7 million bottles, are made from the Mauzac Blanc, a minimum of 15% of the curiously named L'En de l'El (from the local dialect *loin de l'œil*, roughly 'out of sight'), the rest made up with Ondenc, Muscadelle, Sémillon and Sauvignon. They are deliciously aromatic, the dry wines having a good acidity, and should be drunk young. The reds and rosés come from a wide range of grapes: a minimum of 60% must be made up with the Fer, Negrette, Duras, Gamay and Syrah, the rest from the Cabernet Sauvignon, Cabernet Franc, Merlot, Portugais Bleu, Jurançon Rouge and Mauzac. They have a good colour and fruit, some personality, are light and easy to drink and go with anything – the perfect country wine. Many reds are being made by carbonic maceration, and may be drunk young, even *en primeur*, served cool. The best of these particular wines come from Cunac and Labastide-de-Levis. Both red and white wines have a minimum alcohol content of 10.5°, from a yield of 45 hl/ha (which is often exceeded). Most of the production is from Caves Coopératives and prices are very reasonable. Price A – B.

Gaillac doux *AOC*

Sweet white wine subject to the same rules as Gaillac blanc, but with a minimum of 70 grams per litre of residual sugar. These wines are getting more and more rare as the taste for dry wines increases. Price B.

Gaillac Mousseux *AOC*

Sparkling wine from grapes grown in the Gaillac region, made sparkling by the traditional method called *gaillaçoise*. No sugar is added, no *liqueur de tirage* as in the *méthode champenoise*, but fermentation is stopped by successive filtrations, leaving some residual sugar which will produce the sparkle at the secondary fermentation in bottle in the spring following the vintage. The result is a wine with a fine natural sparkle, a delicate bouquet and an attractive softness on the palate. The *méthode champenoise* is in fact used in the region, as it is less risky, but it leaves the wine with less fruit and lacking in charm. Gaillac Mousseux is much appreciated in the local restaurants. Price D.

Gaillac Perlé AOC

Slightly sparkling white wine from the Gaillac region. The wine is fermented at a cool temperature to enhance the bouquet, and is kept for several months on its lees without racking. It is bottled off the lees after malolactic fermentation to retain a slight sparkle that enhances the fruity, refreshing taste. It is delicious as an aperitif or throughout a summer meal. Price C.

Gaillac Premières Côtes AOC

White wine, dry or semi-sweet, from the Gaillac region with a minimum of 12° alcohol from a yield of 40 hl/ha. Very seldom seen, as the wines from Gaillac sell well enough under the less strict *appellation simple*. Price B.

Irouléguy AOC

Red, white and rosé wines from a small vineyard area to the west of Saint-Jean-Pied-de-Port, not far from the Spanish frontier. The whites, in the same style as the Béarn blanc, are virtually non-existent. The reds must be made from the Tannat to a minimum of 50%, the other grapes being the Fer, also indigenous to the South-West, the Cabernet Sauvignon and Cabernet Franc. The minimum alcohol content is 10°, from a yield of 50 hl/ha, and Irouléguy is one of the rare wines in France to have a maximum alcohol level at 14°. The production of rosés dominates that of red, the wine having a pretty orangy-rosé colour (the opposite of the violetty-pink rosés from Bourgueil in the Loire, for example), quite a full flavour and should be drunk young. The reds have more character, an irresistible ruby colour, full of fruit and a spicy *goût de terroir*, without the weight of a Madiran. Both are perfect with the local cuisine, and go very well with egg dishes. Average production is 180,000 bottles a year. Well worth looking out for. Price C.

Jurançon AOC

Sweet white wine from the Pyrénées-Atlantiques, to the south-west of Pau. If, as is common today, the wine is vinified dry, it must be sold under the *appellation* Jurançon sec. The sweet Jurançon, the finest wine from the South-West, famous from the time of

Henri IV, is becoming hard to find as *vignerons* give up the risk of producing a *vin liquoreux*. The vineyards are very parcellated and the local vines – Petit Manseng, Gros Manseng and Courbu – are planted 'high', growing to between 1.5 and 2 metres off the ground, supported by trellises. The very low yield of 25 hl/ha is seldom attained, as the minimum degree of 12.5° is the result of extremely late picking, by which time the grapes have become dried out or raisiny, with the desired concentration of sugar. The wine, with the same weight as a Vouvray Moelleux or a Sauternes, is quite different from these and most individual: the colour is golden, the bouquet rich, honeyed, with hints of nutmeg and cinnamon, even cloves and ginger, the taste luscious with a refreshing lemony acidity in the finish. Jurançon may be drunk young and can be kept for many years.
It is perfect drunk either as an aperitif, with certain hors d'œuvres such as *pâté de foie gras*, or with fruit desserts. It is one of the finest, and most underrated, wines of France. Price D–E.

Jurançon sec *AOC*

Dry white wine from the same region and the same grapes as Jurançon. The permitted yield is double at 50 hl/ha and the minimum alcohol content 11° with a maximum of 12.5°. Jurançon sec, easier to make and to sell than the sweet wine, accounts for about nine-tenths of the average production of 200,000 bottles. The wine is pale in colour, with just a hint of honey and spices on the nose, good clean fruit and a slightly tart finish. It is good as an aperitif or with hors d'œuvres, fish or chicken. The wines from the Coopérative are reliable and inexpensive. Price C–D.

Madiran *AOC*

Red wine from the *départements* of the Pyrénées-Atlantiques, Hautes-Pyrénées and the Gers, to the north-east of Pau and the north-west of Tarbes. Grapes planted are the Tannat (minimum 40%, maximum 60%), the Fer, Cabernet Sauvignon and Cabernet Franc. Minimum alcohol content is 11°, basic maximum yield 45 hl/ha. Madiran rivals Cahors to be the deepest-coloured, longest-lived wine of the South-West. The Tannat makes a wine that is very rough when young, and even if it is tempered with the Cabernet Franc still legally has to spend 20 months in wood before it is bottled. A good Madiran has a splendid purple-ruby colour, a rich, fruity bouquet and a full taste. It is perfect with the local cured ham, excellent with meat and game, unsurpassed with *cassoulet*. It may be drunk at 2 or 3 years but is best between 5 and 10. The wines from the Coopérative are inexpensive, but the growers' wines are better. A classic country wine. Price C–D.

Monbazillac AOC

Sweet and very sweet white wine, from vineyards along the left bank of the Dordogne, to the south of Bergerac. Grape varieties are the same as for Sauternes and the other great sweet wines from the Bordeaux region: Sémillon for flavour and richness, Sauvignon for finesse and body and a little Muscadelle for the heady, slightly muscat aroma. Monbazillac has to have a minimum of 13° alcohol plus residual sugar, from a yield of 40 hl/ha, which is almost never attained, due to the obligatory late harvesting of grapes affected by *botrytis*, where quantity is sacrificed to quality. In good years, Monbazillac is even more rich than a Sauternes, with 14 – 15° natural alcohol and 80 – 100 grams of residual sugar per litre. The wine is enjoying something of a comeback after years of decline, and the wine-makers are paying more attention to see that their wines are clean, not too much sulphured and live up to the fame of the *appellation*. Monbazillac may be drunk young, straw-gold in colour, honeyed and luscious, but it is best kept 5 to 10 years to acquire the complexity that all fine *vins liquoreux* attain with age. Drink very cold, as an aperitif, with *pâté de foie gras* or with fruit-based desserts. Production is large, about 8 million bottles a year, much of it from the Coopérative. A good Monbazillac is extraordinarily good value. Price C – D.

Montravel AOC

Dry, *demi-sec* and sweet white wine from vineyards only 10 kilometres east of Saint-Emilion. Montravel is actually an enclave of the Bordeaux region and it is only because it is in the *département* of the Dordogne that it is not classified among the wines of Bordeaux. Grapes permitted are the Sémillon, Sauvignon and Muscadelle, plus a little Ondenc, Chenin Blanc and Ugni Blanc. The minimum alcohol content is 11°, more if the wine is sweet, from a yield of 50 hl/ha. These are well-made wines, with a light golden colour, soft fruit and a certain charm. Red wine made in Montravel is sold under the *appellation* Bergerac. Good value is to be found from a total production of around 2 million bottles a year. Price B – C.

Pacherenc du Vic Bihl AOC

Dry or slightly sweet white wine from the same region as Madiran. It is made from the local grapes, the Ruffiac, Gros Manseng, Petit Manseng and Courbu, with a little Sémillon and Sauvignon. Minimum alcohol content is 12°, from a yield of 40 hl/ha. The vines are trained high, as at Jurançon, 2 metres above the ground in *pachets-en-rang* (the local dialect for *piquets-en-rang*, 'posts-in-a-line'), hence the name. The wine produced is rich and lively at the same time, not unlike Jurançon, but less luscious, and finishes fruity and slightly honeyed. Good as an aperitif, with hors d'œuvres and especially the local river-fish. Very small production of 90,000 bottles. Price D.

Pécharmant AOC

Red wine from the slopes on the right bank of the Dordogne in the Bergerac region. Grape varieties are limited to Cabernet Sauvignon, Cabernet Franc, Merlot and Malbec. Pécharmant must have a minimum alcohol content of 11°, as opposed to 10° for simple Bergerac, from a maximum yield of 40 hl/ha. The wines are rich in colour, almost purple when young, meaty and generous with a good deal of class. They are at their best at 3 to 6 years, to be drunk with *charcuterie*, white, but preferably red, meats, game and cheese. Pécharmant is the best red wine from the Bergerac region, and is well worth looking out for. Price C–D.

Rosette AOC

Semi-sweet white wine from well-exposed slopes to the north of Bergerac. The Sémillon, Sauvignon and Muscadelle grapes find the limestone-clay soil particularly suitable to producing a wine that is fragrant, delicately sweet but full-bodied and distinctive. Minimum alcohol plus residual sugar is 12°, never more than 15°, from a yield of 40 hl/ha. Not being over-sweet, Rosette is good with fish, poultry and white meats, especially if served with a rich sauce. Production is very small, around 20,000 bottles, and most of it is drunk locally. Price C.

Côtes de Saint-Mont *VDQS*

Red, white and rosé wines from the *département* of the Gers and the eastern Landes. Reds are made from a high proportion (70%) of Tannat, plus Cabernet Sauvignon, Cabernet Franc and Merlot. They have a deep colour and a clean, slightly rough fruit, resembling a more simple version of Madiran. The whites, from the local grapes Meslier, Jurançon, Sauvignon and Picpoul, are pale straw in colour, quite distinctive, dry but not acidic, well worth trying in the local restaurants. Good value. Price A – B.

Côtes du Marmandais *VDQS*

Red and dry white wines from vines planted on either side of the Garonne about 40 kilometres upstream from Langon in the Lot-et-Garonne *département*. The red wine is made from at least 50% 'local' grape varieties: the Fer, Abouriou, Malbec, Gamay and Syrah, the balance being made up by the Bordeaux grapes, Cabernet Sauvignon, Cabernet Franc and Merlot. Minimum alcohol content is 10°, from a yield of 50 hl/ha. Côtes du Marmandais red is pleasant, well balanced with a soft fruit. The very small proportion of white wine is made from the Sauvignon, Ugni Blanc and Sémillon and is dry, pleasantly fruity but sometimes lacking in acidity. Both are unpretentious and inexpensive. Price A – B.

Tursan *VDQS*

Red, dry white and rosé wines from the Landes *département*, around the towns of Geaune and Aire-sur-Adour. The reds and rosés must be made principally from the Tannat grape, with Cabernet Sauvignon, Cabernet Franc and Fer. The wine is solid and well structured, having a minimum of 10.5° alcohol from a yield of 45 hl/ha, quite full in tannin like a minor Madiran. The rosés are simple and fruity, but not so interesting as the reds. The white Tursan, which used to represent most of the production, comes from its own particular grape, the Baroque, to a minimum of 90%. The wine is quite straightforward, having more flavour than bouquet, and goes very well with the local hors d'œuvres and fish. It should be drunk very young. Price B.

Vins d'Entraygues et du Fel VDQS

Red, dry white and rosé wines from the north of the Aveyron *département* and the southern part of the Cantal *département*. The reds and rosés are principally from the Cabernet Sauvignon, Cabernet Franc, Fer, Jurançon Noir, Gamay, Merlot, Negrette and even the Pinot Noir. They are light, with a minimum of 9° alcohol, and fruity, with a pleasing local character. White wines are from the Chenin Blanc and Mauzac, light, with a minimum of 10° alcohol, and attractively crisp. Production is tiny, totalling 6,000 bottles of white, twice that of red and rosé combined, and it is all consumed locally. Price A.

Vins d'Estaing VDQS

Red, dry white and rosé wines from the commune of d'Estaing in the Aveyron *département*. Production of the white wine is insignificant – less than 1,000 bottles a year – from the Chenin Blanc and Mauzac grapes. The reds, from a similar range of grapes to the Vins d'Entraygues et du Fel, are much the same in style: light, fruity and unpretentious. Best drunk on the spot. Price A.

Vins de Lavilledieu VDQS

Red wines (with a minute production of white and rosé), from the *départements* of the Tarn-et-Garonne and Haute-Garonne. The wine is made principally from the Negrette (minimum 35%) plus a wide mixture of varieties, including the Fer, Gamay, Jurançon Noir, Picpoul and Mauzac Noir. The wines resemble those of Gaillac and the Côtes du Frontonnais, pleasant, fruity and slightly rustic. Production is around 10,000 bottles. Price A.

Vins de Marcillac VDQS

Red and rosé wines from around the town of Rodez in the Aveyron *département*. The principal grape planted is the Fer (minimum 80%), the rest being made up by Cabernet, Merlot, Jurançon Noir and Gamay. Marcillac, made almost entirely at the Cave Coopérative, is a deep-coloured, robust, rather rustic wine with lots of fruit. It is good with all *charcuterie*, red meats, stews and cheese. A fine, straightforward country wine. Price B.

Vins de Pays

There are virtually no vins de pays from the Gironde *département*, nor any VDQS. All Bordeaux wines are AOC. In the South-West, however, the old local varieties are often giving way to 'foreign' *cépages* that have no right to an *appellation*, but there has been much replanting. Price A, a few B.

Vins de Pays de la Dordogne

Red, dry white and rosé, the red attractive and fruity, like a Bergerac, the white clean and crisp for everyday drinking.

Vin de Pays de la Gironde

Red and white from the vineyards in the Gironde *département*, not classified as Bordeaux.

Vin de Pays des Landes

Red, dry white and rosé from the south-east of the *département*; red and rosé light in colour and low in alcohol, white straightforward but lacking acidity.

Agenais

Red, dry white and (very little) rosé from the Lot-et-Garonne; red with a deep ruby colour and can be quite tannic, white pale-coloured and fruity with refreshing acidity. The reds travel, the whites do not.

Charentais

Red, dry white and rosé from the Charente and Charente-Maritime; the red wines have a good colour, slight acidity and go well with food; the whites are aromatic and refreshing, with little aftertaste.

Comte Tolosan

Red, dry white and rosé from around Toulouse in the Haute-Garonne and surrounding *départements*. One of the three Vins de Pays Régionaux. Like Côtes du Tarn.

Condomois

Red, dry white and rosé from the Gers. The white is light with good acidity (drink young), the red quite light, best drunk locally (very little rosé is made).

Coteaux de Glanes

Red and rosé from the northern Lot on the left bank of the Dordogne. Light, soft and fruity wines, mostly red.

Coteaux de Quercy

Red and rosé from the Lot below Cahors, and the Tarn-et-Garonne. The Gamay grape makes light, fruity, commercial wines. Excellent table wines, with good colour and definition. The best are those grown around Cahors.

Coteaux et Terrasses de Montauban

Red and rosé from around Montauban in the Tarn-et-Garonne. They have good colour and fruit and in style quite resemble wines of Gaillac.

Côtes de Gascogne

Red, dry white and rosé from the Gers. Very good wines which have started to gain more than a local reputation.

Côtes de Montestruc

Red, dry white and rosé from around Auch in the middle of the Gers *département*. Very like the Côtes de Gascogne (may be sold under its name).

Côtes du Bruhlois

Red and dry white from the Gers and Lot-et-Garonne. The reds are deep-coloured, fruity, slightly rustic, very good with food, the whites very agreeable young.

Côtes du Tarn

Red, dry white and rosé from the western half of the Tarn. These are some of the best *petits vins* from the South-West: the reds brilliant ruby-coloured with good fruit, the rosé very good, the whites everyday wines with some character. These wines are rarely disappointing.

Gorges et Côtes de Millau

Red, dry white and rosé from the Aveyron. Reds quite light in colour, fruity with pleasant acidity, the rosé perhaps better, the whites pale, crisp, with distinctive fruit and good acidity. Their quality puts them into the VDQS category.

Saint-Sardon

Red, dry white and rosé from west of Montauban in the Tarn-et-Garonne and the north-west corner of the Haute-Garonne. Reds and rosés are easy to drink, whites resemble the minor dry whites from Bordeaux.

The Loire Valley

Virtually every style of wine is to be found in the Loire Valley, from the driest whites to rich, honeyed dessert wines, from light, fruity reds to be drunk young, to more serious reds to be treated like Claret, the complete range of rosés, and the second most famous sparkling wine in France. Many, indeed most, are perfect 'local' wines, delicious to drink on the spot, yet requested the world over.

The river Loire rises in the Auvergne, on the same latitude as the Beaujolais, so it is not surprising to find the Gamay grape widely planted, making characteristically fruity wines with a discernible *goût de terroir*. As the river winds northwards, the white Burgundy grapes Chardonnay and Aligoté are seen alongside the Sauvignon, and the Pinot Noir makes one of its rare appearances outside the Côte d'Or to make wines at Saint-Pourçain that are not yet typically Loire in style. The wines become more what we expect as the river enters the Nivernais, with Pouilly-Fumé and Sancerre and the similar-tasting Quincy and Reuilly. Further north still, very little wine is now made around Gien, where a century ago there were 800 *vignerons*. Even the vines around Orléans are being engulfed by the city itself.

When the river turns left towards the sea, entering the château country, vines begin in earnest and are planted with hardly a break right up to the mouth of the Loire at Nantes. The white wines of Touraine witness the change from Sauvignon to Chenin Blanc, while the Pinot Noir, still in evidence at Sancerre, disappears in favour of the

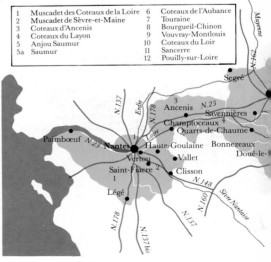

1	Muscadet des Coteaux de la Loire	6	Coteaux de l'Aubance
2	Muscadet de Sèvre-et-Maine	7	Touraine
3	Coteaux d'Ancenis	8	Bourgueil-Chinon
4	Coteaux du Layon	9	Vouvray-Montlouis
5	Anjou Saumur	10	Coteaux du Loir
5a	Saumur	11	Sancerre
		12	Pouilly-sur-Loire

Cabernet family. Attractive, mostly white, wines are made around Cheverny and Chambord; Amboise produces some good wines under the *appellation* Touraine, while the finest wines in this part are from the region of Tours. From the east come Montlouis and Vouvray, similar white wines both made from the Chenin Blanc, with the ability to be bone-dry, *demi-sec*, lusciously rich or sparkling. From the west, on the outskirts of the Saumurois, come the best red wines in the Loire Valley, Chinon and Bourgueil, made from the Cabernet Franc.

As the river enters the province of Anjou, the style changes again. With the exception of the excellent wines from Saumur Champigny, red wines become less interesting, although they are still typically Loire in style, fruity and slightly rustic. The rosés, dry or *demi-sec*, are well known and popular, but the white wines of Bonnezeaux, Coteaux du Layon and Quarts de Chaume are the jewels of the Loire, honey-sweet, long underrated and only now coming back into fashion. The dry whites, also from the Chenin Blanc, are good, especially at Savennières.

The Pays Nantais bring another change in style. Here the wines are dry and almost exclusively white. There are some pleasant reds and rosés made at Ancenis, but the well-known wine here is the Muscadet, the pale, almost cracklingly crisp white wine that is synonymous with shellfish throughout the world, a perfect country wine Even drier than Muscadet, and often too tart for most tastes, is the Gros Plant du Pays Nantais.

The four regions are looked at from west to east.

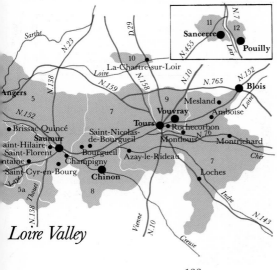

Loire Valley

The Wines of the Atlantic Coast and the West

This region is dominated by the wines from the Muscadet region. These light, crisp, slightly acidic wines have a tanginess that has more in common with Brittany than the Loire Valley. All wines – red, white and rosé – from this part of the Loire Valley are light, low in alcohol, and should be drunk young.

The Muscadet region

Muscadet is the name of the grape variety as well as the name of the wine. The grape originated in Burgundy, where it was called 'le Melon de Bourgogne' because of the rounded form of its leaves, and where it is now no longer planted. The name 'Muscadet' probably comes from the slightly 'musky' flavour of the wine. Muscadet is the archetypal dry white wine: harvested early to keep the freshness and fruit, very pale in colour, dry but not acid, with a certain finesse and charm and a well-defined character. It goes perfectly with shellfish, and well with hors d'œuvres and fish, white meats and even goat's cheese. As a popular wine, its only rival is Beaujolais. The annual production of Muscadet is around 65 million bottles, which is divided between three *appellations*.

Muscadet AOC

Dry white wine only from the Muscadet grape; minimum alcohol content 9.5°, maximum 12°. Yield 50 hl/ha. Drink as young as possible. The label may add *sur lie* (bottled on its lees) to the *appellation*, if the wine has not been racked off its lees after fermentation and if it is bottled before the next vintage. In fact, most Muscadets are bottled before the summer. The production of Muscadet *tout court* represents not more than 10% of the *appellation*. Price B.

Muscadet des Coteaux de la Loire AOC

From vines planted on the right bank of the Loire, up-river from Nantes towards Ancenis. Minimum alcohol content is 10°, otherwise the same conditions as for Muscadet apply. The wine is clean and fruity, possibly a little fuller in style than Muscadet *tout court*, but rather more tart and less flavourful than Muscadet de Sèvre-et-Maine. It represents not more than 5% of the total production. Drink young. Price B.

Muscadet de Sèvre-et-Maine AOC

From south-east of Nantes, in the Sèvre-et-Maine *département*. The best Muscadet wines come from this region with its rolling hills and stony-clayey soil. Same conditions as above. The finest wine comes from the cantons of Vallet, Clisson and Loroux-Bottereau, delicate, with much finesse and great length of flavour. Drink young, but can be most enjoyable at 2 to 4 years. Price B–C.

Coteaux d'Ancenis VDQS

Little-known red, dry white and rosé wines from the right bank of the Loire around Ancenis. The label must state the name of the grape from which the wine is made:

Pineau de la Loire, Chenin Blanc, Pinot Beurot and Malvoisie (white); Gamay and Cabernet Franc (red and rosé). With the exception of wine from the Malvoisie, which can be slightly sweet, the Coteaux d'Ancenis are light, dry, fruity and refreshing, best drunk when young on picnics or with hors d'œuvres, light fish or meat. Minimum alcohol content 10°, yield 40 hl/ha. Price B.

Gros Plant du Pays Nantais VDQS

Dry white wine grown from the grape of the same name, also known as the Folle-Blanche, which originated in the Cognac region, directly to the south. Gros Plant is 'greener' than Muscadet and appears drier, and should be drunk very young as an aperitif or with shellfish. Minimum alcohol content 9°, yield 50 hl/ha. Price B.

The Wines of Anjou and the Saumurois

The ancient royal province of Anjou corresponds roughly to what the *département* of the Maine-et-Loire is today. Vines are planted along the banks of the Loire and its tributaries and benefit from clear light and temperate climate. The wines of Anjou have a reputation stretching back to the twelfth century, and while, historically, the white wines are the most sought after, offering a complete range of styles from bone-dry to honey-sweet and even sparkling, there are some excellent red wines being produced as well as the ever-popular rosés.

The wines of Saumur have a reputation as old as those of Anjou and, while they are officially classified with Anjou, they have perhaps more in common with the wines of Touraine. The white wines are generally dry or *demi-sec*, with sweet wines being made in only the best years. The soil, a hard chalky-clay known as *le tuffeau*, produces long-lasting wines of great character. Vines grown on a more sandy soil are fine, but lighter. The region around the town of Saumur itself is particularly well known for sparkling wines made by the *méthode champenoise*, while the red wine made at Champigny can claim to be the finest in the Loire.

Anjou AOC

anjou

Appellation Contrôlée

CONSEIL INTERPROFESSIONNEL DES VINS D'ANJOU ET DE SAUMUR
21, BOULEVARD FOCH, 49000 ANGERS

Red, white and rosé wines mainly from the *département* of the Maine-et-Loire, but also from parts of the *départements* of Deux-Sèvres and the Vienne. Within these geographical limits, wines may be made from the following grapes: Reds: Cabernet Franc, Cabernet Sauvignon, Pineau d'Aunis. Rosés: Cabernet Franc, Cabernet Sauvignon, Pineau d'Aunis, Gamay, Cot, Groslot. Whites: Chenin Blanc (Pineau de la Loire) to a minimum of 80%, with a maximum of 20% made up by Chardonnay or Sauvignon.

Anjou is the global *appellation* that covers several regional or communal *appellations* (see below) as the *appellation* Bourgogne covers Pommard, Nuits-Saint-Georges and so on. The white wines are generally dry, with a soft, honeysuckle fruit in good years, the rosés are light in colour, charming, often with a touch of sweetness and the reds have a good colour, lots of fruit and a delightful, if rather rustic *goût de terroir*. There are around 52,000 hectares in production, with a basic yield of 50 hl/ha. Price C, but very much more for the high-quality sweet whites.

Anjou Coteaux de la Loire AOC

White wines only, dry and semi-sweet from both sides of the Loire around Angers. The vineyard area is small, but well exposed; only the Pineau de la Loire may be planted, producing a wine with a bouquet of summer flowers and a discreet fruit flavour, to be drunk on its own, or with light entrées and white meat.

The *demi-sec* is softer and slightly honeyed, but not as intense as the sweet wines from the Coteaux de l'Aubance or Coteaux du Layon. The minimum alcohol content is quite high at 12°, with a low yield of 30 hl/ha; no marked acidity. These are wines to drink young. Price C–D.

Anjou Gamay AOC

Mostly red wines made from the Gamay grape on its own and required to say so on the label. Light, easy to drink, less interesting than red Anjou from the Cabernet, but attractive when drunk young and cool. Price B–C.

Anjou Mousseux AOC

Very small production of white and rosé wines made sparkling by the *méthode champenoise*. The principal grape is Pineau de la Loire, but up to 60% of Cabernet, Gamay, Cot, Groslot and Pineau d'Aunis may be added to the press to make the white wine. The sparkling wines from Saumur are more popular. Price D.

Bonnezeaux AOC

BONNEZEAUX
APPELLATION BONNEZEAUX CONTRÔLÉE
CHATEAU DE FESLE

Mise en bouteille à la Propriété
J. BOIVIN, Propriétaire THOUARCÉ (M. & Loire) FRANCE

Situated on the right bank of the river Layon in the commune of Thouarcé, Bonnezeaux is a *grand cru* of the *appellation* Coteaux du Layon, and, alongside the other *grand cru appellation* Quarts de Chaume, produces the finest sweet white wines in Anjou. Only the Pineau de la Loire (Chenin Blanc) is planted, and the bunches of grapes are left on the vines until late October to await the *pourriture noble*. In good years Bonnezeaux is rich and perfumed, with an unctuous fruit but a refreshing lemony acidity that prevents it becoming cloying. It can be drunk young, in the year after the vintage while it is still exploding with fruit, and it ages beautifully. It is naturally sweet and high in alcohol (minimum 13.5° total after fermentation) and is perfect as an aperitif, with fish in a cream sauce, with fruit desserts or in the middle of a summer's afternoon. Production is small. Price E, and F for older vintages.

Cabernet d'Anjou
Cabernet d'Anjou-Val-de-Loire AOC

Semi-sweet rosés from the Anjou region, made from the Cabernet Franc and/or Cabernet Sauvignon grapes exclusively. Minimum alcohol required is 10°, plus 10 grams per litre residual sugar; yield 40 hl/ha, average production per year 1.2 million bottles. This prettily coloured, semi-sweet rosé enjoyed a great success from the 1890s to the 1950s, when (not helped by rather poor wine-making overall) this style of wine began to lose favour. If well made and drunk young, they have a soft salmon-pink colour, violetty or raspberry bouquet and a *tendre* finish. Best drunk on its own, quite cold, or with petits fours. Price C–D.

Cabernet de Saumur AOC

Semi-sweet rosés from the Saumur region, with the same *appellation* conditions as the Cabernet d'Anjou. The colour is perhaps paler, often as light as a *vin gris*, and the taste a little lighter and firmer, less rich. Small production, around 120,000 bottles. Price C–D.

Coteaux de l'Aubance AOC

Semi-sweet and sweet white wines from vines grown along the banks of the river Aubance, a tributary of the Loire. These soft, charming, fruity wines are grown on the same schistous soil as the Coteaux du Layon and from the same grape (Chenin Blanc), and are similar in character but less intense in flavour. The yield is low, 30 hl/ha, and the production declining in favour of dry whites made from the Chenin Blanc or reds and rosés made from the Cabernet or Gamay, which are more popular, but have only the right to the *appellation* Anjou. Price D (Coteaux de l'Aubance); C (Anjou).

Coteaux de Saumur AOC

Tiny production (12,000 bottles) of *demi-sec* white wine from Chenin Blanc grapes grown on the *tuffeau* soil of the Saumur region. Not unlike the wines of Vouvray: a bouquet of honey and flowers, followed by crisp, well-defined fruit flavours. It is almost all drunk locally. Price D.

Coteaux du Layon AOC

Semi-sweet and sweet white wines grown along the banks of the Layon from the Pineau de la Loire (Chenin Blanc) exclusively. Dry whites and rosés from the upper reaches of the Layon go under the *appellation* Anjou, or Rosé d'Anjou. After very late harvesting of grapes attacked by *pourriture noble*, wines from this region have a greeny-golden colour, a flowery, honeyed bouquet and a richness on the palate tempered by the Pineau's natural acidity. They are in the same category as, but lighter (12° minimum alcohol plus sugar) than, the Sauternes or Barsacs from Bordeaux. The best communes – Beaulieu, Faye, Rablay, Rochefort, Saint-Aubin-de-Luigné – may add their name after Coteaux du Layon if the wine is richer and more intense (13° minimum, of which 12° is natural), while the communes of Quarts de Chaume and Bonnezeaux have their own *appellations*. They should be drunk cold, but not iced which stuns the delicate flavour. The production is quite large and, if a tendency to over-sulphur during vinification or bottling is avoided, the wines are very fine and good value for money. Price D–E.

Coteaux du Layon-Chaume AOC

The same style and character as above, with the grapes coming exclusively from the commune of Rochefort-sur-Loire and minimum total alcohol content 13°. Only a handful of *vignerons* use this *appellation*. Price D–E.

Crémant de Loire AOC

White and rosé wines from the accepted grape varieties grown in the Anjou, Saumur and Touraine regions, made sparkling by the *méthode champenoise*. A crémant is less 'bubbly' than a fully sparkling wine, with an atmospheric pressure of 3.5 kg as opposed to 5 kg. Price D.

Quarts de Chaume AOC

Sweet, generally luscious white wines from the Pineau de la Loire grape. Quarts de Chaume is, with Bonnezeaux, a *grand cru* of Coteaux du Layon. The wines are in the same style: a very late harvest of over-ripe grapes attacked by *pourriture noble*, producing a luscious wine with a honeyed, sometimes apricot, explosively floral bouquet, rich on the palate, with a hint of bitterness in the finish which only accentuates the finesse of the whole. The production is very small, 22 hl/ha over only 40 hectares, making only 100,000 bottles in good years. Quarts de Chaume is delicious even in light years, and in good years can rival the finest sweet wines in the world. Price E–F.

Rosé d'Anjou AOC

Slightly sweet rosés made from any or all of the red wine varieties planted in Anjou: Cabernet Franc, Cabernet Sauvignon, Pineau d'Aunis, Gamay, Cot and Groslot. They are light in alcohol (9° minimum), with a minimum of 9 grams per litre residual sugar, very pretty to look at and refreshing to drink. Best drunk on their own, at the start of a meal or throughout a summer's lunch. The same yield as Anjou: 50 hl/ha. Price B–C.

Rosé d'Anjou Pétillant AOC

The still rosé from Anjou, made *pétillant* by the *méthode champenoise*. This is a lengthy and expensive process, and since the demand for semi-sweet, semi-sparkling rosés is small, this wine is hardly made any more. Price C.

Rosé de Loire AOC

A dry rosé made in Anjou, Saumur and Touraine. Same grapes as the Rosé d'Anjou, but the Cabernets must represent a minimum of 30%, and not more than 3 grams per litre residual sugar is allowed. It is lighter, brisker than the Anjou; most of the production of 2.5 million bottles is made in Touraine. Price B–C.

Saumur AOC

White, both dry and sweet, and red wines made from the same grapes as are the red and white wines of Anjou. The dry white wines, with a minimum of 10° alcohol and a yield of 45 hl/ha, are very fine, clean, fruity, harmonious and last well. The difference between Saumur and Anjou is the chalky-clayey *tuffeau* soil, which produces wines more in the style of Vouvray. They are delicious with hors d'œuvres, fish and light meat dishes, particularly pork. The sweeter wines from Saumur come under the *appellation* Coteaux de Saumur. The red wines, quite low in alcohol (10° minimum) with a low yield of 40 hl/ha, may be light in colour, but are straightforward, fruity and pleasantly regional in character. The finest of these wines come from Saumur-Champigny, which has its own *appellation*. Over two-thirds of wines produced in Saumur are white. Price C (red); D (white).

Saumur-Champigny AOC

The best red wine in the Saumurois and Anjou. Already well known in the Middle Ages, the wines from Champigny resemble Bourgueil and Chinon from Touraine, but are a little sturdier. They have an exciting, deep colour (purple when young) from the Cabernet grape, a concentrated fruity-earthy aroma of raspberries or wild strawberries, with a smoothness and generosity on the palate backed up by a firm finish. They may be drunk young, one or two years after the vintage, served at cellar temperature, or kept for 5 to 10 years. Like so many wines from the Loire, particularly the reds, they taste immeasurably better on the spot with the local cuisine. Price C–D, very good value.

Saumur Mousseux *AOC*

White and rosé sparkling wines. The whites, since they are made by the *méthode champenoise*, may include the permitted red grapes in the *cuvée* to a maximum of 60%. If Chardonnay or Sauvignon is used, it must be to a maximum of 20%, the rest being Chenin Blanc. The *méthode champenoise* involves the addition of alcohol (*liqueur de tirage*) to encourage the secondary fermentation, so wines to be made into Saumur Mousseux may be as low as 8.5° from a high yield of 60 hl/ha. In any event, wines high in alcohol do not make good sparkling wines. They are mostly sold under brand names (Gratien et Meyer, Langlois Château, Ackermann, etc.), as are the majority of Champagnes. Either *crémant* or fully sparkling, they are fine quality sparkling wines and are justifiably successful. The production of rosé is about 5% of the total. Price D.

Saumur Pétillant *AOC*

These wines have virtually ceased to exist, since, although made in the same way as Saumur Mousseux, they could not legally use the Champagne *habillage* or presentation (Champagne cork held in place by wire, silver foil around the neck, etc.), and had to look like a still wine. Those wines which are produced are very much appreciated locally. Price probably D.

Savennières *AOC*

Dry and semi-sweet white wines, the finest in the Saumurois. The vines are situated on the right bank of the Loire, around the village of Savennières, and are planted on steep slopes that run down to the river, superbly exposed. Made exclusively from the Pineau de la Loire (Chenin Blanc), with a minimum concentration of alcohol and sugar of 12.5° from a very low yield of 25 hl/ha, these wines are elegant, with delicacy and finesse overlaying the firm aromatic fruit. They are generally dry, with a good acidity that allows them to age well, perfect with river-fish or chicken. In good years with a lot of sun they have a concentration of sugar that makes them richer but never sweet. Production is small, under 200,000 bottles. Price D and E for a late-picked wine or older vintage.

Savennières-Coulée-de-Serrant AOC
Savennières-Roche-aux-Moines AOC

The two *grands crus* of the Savennières *appellation*. These are very fine wines, the *monopole* la Coulée de Serrant being exceptional. This cannot really be called a country wine, even though it is drunk locally. Price F.

Vins du Haut Poitou VDQS

Vins du Haut Poitou
APPELLATION D'ORIGINE VINS DÉLIMITÉS DE QUALITÉ SUPÉRIEURE
Mis en bouteille à la propriété
Ñd Sauvignon
CCHP 86170 NEUVILLE-DE-POITOU FRANCE

Red, dry white (still and sparkling) and rosé wines mostly from the Vienne *département* around Poitiers. Whites are from the Sauvignon, Chardonnay, Pinot Blanc and Chenin Blanc (to a maximum of 20%, the opposite of what pertains in Anjou). Reds and rosés are made principally from the Gamay, Pinot Noir, Cabernet Sauvignon, Chardonnay, Pinot Blanc and Chenin Blanc, Cot and Groslot (also known as Grolleau). The wines are light in both colour and body (whites and rosés 9.5° alcohol, reds 9°), fresh, fruity and should be drunk young and chilled. The Sauvignon and the Gamay are typical of their grape varietal and are very popular, and the Chardonnay is crisp and distinctive. Price B–C.

Vins du Thouarsais VDQS

Red, dry white and rosé wines from around Bressuire in the Deux-Sèvres *département*. The white is made from Chenin Blanc, the reds and rosés from Cabernet Sauvignon and Cabernet Franc. These are quite light (9.5° minimum alcohol for the whites, 9° for the reds), pleasant, fruity wines in the Anjou style, but simpler. Drink young and cool, even the reds. Price B.

The Wines of Touraine

The province of Touraine is known as 'the garden of France', and its wines were esteemed even before those of Anjou. The styles are similar to those in Anjou and the Saumurois, the climate ideal and the soil, whether it be the chalky-clay *tuffeau* or the sandy-gravelly alluvial plains, perfect for the vine. The Pineau de la Loire is at its best and most diverse in Touraine, while the Cabernet Franc (le Breton) and the Gamay produce the most attractive reds and rosés. Touraine is at the centre of the Loire Valley and represents, more concisely than the other provinces, *les vins de la Loire* at their most typical and distinctive.

Bourgueil AOC

Red and rosé wines made from the Cabernet Franc and Cabernet Sauvignon, but principally the former. All other red grapes found in Touraine are excluded. Minimum alcohol content is 9.5°, and the yield 40 hl/ha. There are two different types of soil in the Bourgueil region, that produce two styles of wine: the gravelly, alluvial soil produces wines that are lighter, have more finesse and more bouquet and are ready to drink early; the chalky-clay *tuffeau* produces wines that are bigger, firmer and need time to mature. In many cases, the two styles are blended, with great success. Bourgueil has a deep, ruby colour, violet when young, a marvellous bouquet of raspberries and a refreshingly clean taste not unlike a Médoc. It can be drunk young, at cellar temperature, the year after the vintage, while the best wines last 10 years or more. With Saumur-Champigny and Chinon, Bourgueil is the finest red wine from the Loire. The rosé has a pretty violetty-pink colour, much charm and finesse, and is pleasantly dry. Price C – D.

Chinon AOC

Red, dry white and rosé wines grown on the left bank of the Loire and on both banks of the river Vienne. The white is very rare, under 1% of the total production, comes from the Pineau de la Loire, and is clean and fruity but often rather acidic. Almost none is exported. The red is made principally from the Cabernet Franc, known locally as 'le Breton'. It is very similar to Bourgueil, which is grown on the other side of the Loire, and the same different types of soil – *gravier* and *tuffeau*, which make the lighter and the firmer styles of wine. Chinon has a lovely ruby colour, a distinctive aroma of violets and a clean fruity finish. In general it is a little softer than Bourgueil and may be drunk quite young, while wine from good years or old vines have more depth and last longer. Drink at cellar temperature, to enhance the fruit. A little rosé is made, prettily coloured and dry, from the Cabernet Franc. Chinon should never be heavy or lacking in charm. Minimum alcohol content 9.5°, yield 40 hl/ha, average production 5 million bottles. Chinon is better known than the *appellations* Bourgueil and Saint-Nicolas, and is therefore a little more expensive. Price C – D – E.

Coteaux du Loir AOC

Red, dry white and rosé wines grown on the slopes of both banks of the river Loir, about 40 kilometres north of Tours. Although historically these vineyards were as well known as any in Touraine, they are virtually extinct today, with only 20 hectares under vines. The whites are made from the Pineau de la Loire (Chenin Blanc), and resemble the wines from Vouvray, but with a bit more acidity; the reds may be made from the Pineau d'Aunis, Gamay, Cabernet Franc and Cot and have a good colour and are well made and fruity, if slightly rustic in character; rosés may be made with the same grapes, plus up to 25% of Groslot. The whites age well, owing to the acidity, while the reds and rosés should be drunk young. All three styles of wine go very well with the local *rillettes*. Price C.

Crémant de Loire AOC

See under Anjou, page 139.

Jasnières AOC

White wine from the global *appellation* Coteaux du Loir, but which must come from the communes of Lhomme and Ruillé-sur-Loir. Made from the Pineau de la Loire, the minimum alcohol content is 10° and the yield very small at 25 hl/ha. The wine produced has great delicacy, finesse and character, and at its best Jasnières is the equal of the finest wines in Touraine. Although in poor years it is rather green and acidic, in great years it acquires vanilla-honeyed aromas and a natural sweetness. Difficult climatic conditions combined with the low yield impose a severe financial burden on the small number of *vignerons* who still make the very rare Jasnières. Price D.

Montlouis AOC

White wines, either dry or sweet, from the left bank of the Loire, opposite the vineyards of Vouvray. The wine is made from the Pineau de la Loire, and the soil, methods of cultivation and vinification are so similar to the wines made on the other bank that, until 1938, Montlouis was sold as Vouvray. Wines from this *appellation* may be dry, *demi-sec*, fully sweet or *liquoreux*, semi-sparkling and sparkling. The still wines are the most interesting, with the fresh, honeysuckle aromas of the Pineau de la Loire, the great finesse of the *terroir* and the lemon-fruit finish. They may be drunk soon after the vintage, but keep for several years. Montlouis is an underrated wine, not even popular enough to attract purchases by *négociants* except to be made into sparkling wine. Very little is exported, and it is well worth looking out for in France, locally or in Paris. Price C–D.

Montlouis Mousseux AOC

Montlouis still wine (9.5° minimum alcohol, yield 45 hl/ha), made sparkling by the *méthode champenoise*. Production is about five times that of the still wines, around 3.5 million bottles, since *vins mousseux* are very popular in France, and sparkling Montlouis justifiably so. It is usually *brut*, but may be *sec*, *demi-sec* or *moelleux*. Price D.

Montlouis Pétillant AOC

White semi-sparkling wines from Montlouis. As the *appellation* suggests, they are only slightly effervescent, and reflect more of the original quality of the still wine. Very little is made, yet it makes a superb aperitif. Price D.

Rosé de Loire AOC

See under Anjou, page 140.

Saint-Nicolas-de-Bourgueil AOC

Red and rosé wines from the Cabernet Franc grape, although Cabernet Sauvignon may also be planted. Very similar in style to Bourgueil, but the permitted yield is less at 35 hl/ha, and Saint-Nicolas is considered to have the edge over Bourgueil when it comes to finesse. Should be drunk at cellar temperature, but not too cold. Apart from exceptional vintages, Saint-Nicolas is at its best at 2 to 5 years. Price C–D.

Touraine AOC

Dry, semi-sweet and sweet white wines, red and rosé wines made in the *départements* of Indre-et-Loire, Loir-et-Cher and a very little in the Indre. The permitted grape varieties are: White wines: Pineau de la Loire (Chenin Blanc), Menu-Pineau (or Arbois), Sauvignon and Chardonnay, which is limited to 20% of the area planted.
Red wines: Cabernet Franc (Breton), Cabernet Sauvignon, Cot, Pinot Meunier, Pinot Gris, Pineau d'Aunis, Gamay.
Rosés: as above, plus the Groslot.

The minimum alcohol content is 9° for the reds and 9.5° for the whites and rosés, from a basic yield of 45 hl/ha. The Sauvignon is planted to the east of the *appellation*, as is the Gamay. These fresh young wines, packed with fruit, are often seen under the names 'Sauvignon de Touraine' and 'Gamay de Touraine', to benefit from both the popularity of the grape varieties and the regional *appellation*. They are an excellent, and less expensive, alternative to the Sauvignons from the centre of France and the Gamays from the Beaujolais. The name of an individual commune may be added to Touraine on the label, if the wines are particularly distinctive.

Around 35 million bottles of wine are produced annually in Touraine, the style following more the grape variety than the actual *appellation*. The Chenin Blanc has much in common with the Saumur whites, and finds the best expression of its honeysuckle-lemony fruit in the wines of Vouvray. The roses are drier than in Anjou, perhaps more elegant as well. The reds made from the Breton (Cabernet Franc) are important wines of great fragrance and fruit, while those made from the minor varieties are simpler, 'country wines' personified. Prices B (very few), C–D.

Touraine-Amboise AOC

White, red and rosé wines from the same grape varieties as Touraine, but grown around Amboise. These wines must have one more degree of alcohol than the Touraine *tout court*, hence more concentration of flavour. The whites are generally dry, with a pale greeny-gold colour, soft fruit and good acidity. They can age well and are at their best with hors d'œuvres, especially pâtés, fish, white meats and goat's cheese. The rosés are attractive and fruity and the reds are slightly rough and acidic, but go well with food. Prices C, well worth looking for.

Touraine-Azay-le-Rideau AOC

A small production of white and rosé wines. The wines are made from the Pineau de la Loire, and the rosés must have a minimum of 60% Grolleau (or Groslot) in their make-up, with 40% coming from other varieties. Both wines may be very slightly sweet, and are excellent for picnics, light lunches and everyday drinking. They do not taste as good away from the local cuisine. Price C.

Touraine-Mesland AOC

White, red and rosé wines as found in the *appellation* Touraine, but grown in the region of Mesland. The extra natural degree of alcohol gives these wines an extra degree of character and style, as it does to the Touraine-Amboise. Mesland produces wines which are slightly higher in acidity than Amboise, but with as much, if not more, personality. The wines are generally made from single grape varieties: Chenin, Sauvignon, Cabernet, Gamay, even Cot, and will mention this on the label. Each varietal is distinctive, the Chenin and the Cabernet producing the more typical Touraine style. Price C.

Touraine Mousseux AOC

All white and rosé wines that are in the Touraine *appellation* may be made sparkling by the *méthode champenoise*. The reds have to come from the *appellations* Bourgueil, Saint-Nicolas-de-Bourgueil and Chinon, of which none is nowadays sold as *mousseux*. In fact, this *appellation* has been largely replaced by the Crémant de Touraine, which sells under the *appellation* Touraine. It is very agreeable, but less good than a Vouvray. Price D.

Touraine Pétillant AOC

The same rules apply as above, except that as for Saumur Pétillant, the bottles may not be confused with those made and presented like Champagne, which makes them impossible to sell on the export market. The wine is still made and drunk locally. Price D.

Vouvray AOC

White wine made from the Pineau de la Loire on the right bank of the Loire to the east of Tours. Vouvray may be *brut*, *sec*, *demi-sec*, *moelleux*, *liquoreux*, semi-sparkling or sparkling, depending on the decision of the wine-maker and, especially for the sweet wines where the grapes have to have been affected by *pourriture noble*, on the quality of the year. The wine must have a minimum alcohol content of 11° from a yield of 45 hl/ha, which gives it a certain structure without spoiling the delicacy and finesse. A dry Vouvray of good quality has the explosive honeysuckle aromas of the Pineau, a clean, satisfying fruit flavour and good acidity. The sweeter wines have more intense floral aromas, a honeyed, sometimes apricot finish, but should not be cloying. The dry and *demi-sec* wines are lovely as an aperitif, with hors d'œuvres, and are really quite superb with the local salmon or pike. They may be drunk young but, in common with all fine wines from the Pineau de la Loire grape, they age beautifully. The sweeter wines are best enjoyed on their own, with fresh summer fruit and possibly with *pâté de foie gras*.

At their best they are as luscious and complex as the finest Sauternes, and can last for as long as 50 years. Price D for a recent vintage; E for more mature wines; F for the finest bottles.

Vouvray Mousseux AOC

White wine from the Vouvray region with a minimum of 9.5° alcohol before the

addition of the *liqueur de tirage*, made sparkling by the *méthode champenoise*. Depending on the *dosage*, sparkling Vouvray may be *brut*, *sec*, *demi-sec* and very rarely *moelleux*. If red grapes are planted in Vouvray, they carry the *appellation* Touraine, and some proprietors make a delightful sparkling Touraine rosé. Sparkling Vouvray is one of the best alternatives to Champagne, but is mostly drunk on its own merits. Price D–E.

Vouvray Pétillant AOC

White wine from vineyards in the Vouvray region, less sparkling than the Vouvray

Mousseux. Since the flavour of the wine is of more importance than its bubbliness, Vouvray Pétillant is particularly agreeable, as none of the quality of the wine (or lack of it) is covered up by the sparkle, but merely enhanced by the slight effervescence. Very little Pétillant is made and most of it is drunk in the local restaurants. Price D.

Cheverny VDQS

Red, white and rosé wines produced in the region of Cheverny, to the south of Blois, in the *département* of Loir-et-Cher. This is one of the relatively new VDQS *appellations*, whose wines are of generally high quality and very typically 'Loire' in style. The whites are made from the Chenin Blanc, Sauvignon, Menu-Pineau (or Arbois), Chardonnay and Romorantin (very rare, and rather unyieldingly acid for most tastes). They are very attractive, fresh, fruity wines to be drunk young. The grape is usually specified on the label, the Chenin Blanc resembling a light Touraine and the very popular Sauvignon a minor Sancerre. The reds may be made from the Gamay, Cabernet Franc or Cabernet Sauvignon, Pinot Noir or Cot, and these grapes may be vinified as rosés, as may the Pineau d'Aunis and Pinot Gris. Both reds and rosés are light in colour and body (minimum alcohol content 9°, as opposed to 9.5° for the whites, both from a yield of 50 hl/ha) and are to be drunk young, especially the Cheverny-Gamay. A little sparkling wine is made by the *méthode champenoise*, mostly for local consumption. The *vignerons* in this *appellation* are serious and very proud of their VDQS status. The wines, with their honest fruit and crisp natural acidity, represent very good value for money. Price B.

Coteaux du Vendômois *VDQS*

Red, white and rosé wines from vineyards planted in the commune of Vendôme in the *département* of Loir-et-Cher.

The white grape is the Chenin Blanc, with Chardonnay admitted up to 20%, Pineau d'Aunis and Gamay for the rosés, to which may be added Pinot Noir and Cabernet for the reds. White wine represents only 10% of the total production. The reds have a pretty ruby colour and a soft fruit, and should be drunk young. They are attractive, minor wines. Price B.

Valençay *VDQS*

Dry white, red and rosé wines from the region of Valençay in the *département* of the Indre. The *encépagement* is not classic Touraine, with 60% minimum Menu-Pineau (Arbois), the rest made up from Sauvignon, Chardonnay, Pineau de la Loire and Romorantin. The style is clean and firm with good fruit, but perhaps less flowery than the other Touraine whites from the Pineau de la Loire. The reds are more than three-quarters made from Cabernet Sauvignon, Cabernet Franc, Cot, Gamay and Pineau d'Aunis. They are light in alcohol, 9° minimum, but have good fruit and local character. Four-fifths of the total production is red or rosé. These wines are delightful drunk on the spot, but taste a little thin away from home. Price B.

Wines of the Centre and the East

While the wines from these regions are as delightful and diverse as those from the more western parts of the Loire Valley, there are notable differences in style. For white wines, the Pineau de la Loire gives way to the Sauvignon, while for reds and rosés, the Cabernet disappears in favour of the Pinot Noir and the Gamay. To the north are the wines of Orléans, now much better known for its vinegar, and the light wines around Gien. Up-river, but to the south, are the famous wines of Sancerre and Pouilly-Fumé, as well known as Vouvray and Muscadet, and the similar but lesser-known Quincy, Reuilly and Ménétou-Salon. Following the river, and its tributaries the Cher and the Allier, to their source, the style changes to the more simple wines of the Auvergne, which seem to have more in common with Burgundy than the Loire Valley.

Blanc Fumé de Pouilly or Pouilly-Fumé AOC

Dry white wine made exclusively from the Sauvignon grape on the right bank of the Loire around the town of Pouilly-sur-Loire. The Sauvignon, known locally as the 'Blanc Fumé', must produce wines with a minimum alcohol content of 11° from a maximum yield of 45 hl/ha. The wine is generally excellent, pale in colour sometimes with a greenish tinge, a subtle bouquet in which blackcurrant leaf, redcurrants and spiciness are mixed, and a long, elegant finish. The 'smokiness' from the grape is apparent in a slightly musky aroma. Pouilly-Fumé can be too tart in poor years, is normally drunk one or two years after the vintage, but is capable of softening out while retaining its freshness for 4 or 5 years. It is perfect with river-fish and very good as an aperitif or with white meats. With an average production of 3 million bottles (less than half that of Sancerre), and a risk of spring frosts, Pouilly-Fumé is much in demand. Price D–E.

Ménétou-Salon AOC

White, red and rosé wines from vines grown around the village of Ménétou-Salon in the Cher *département* north of Bourges. The whites, from the Sauvignon grape grown on the same chalky soils as at Sancerre, are in the same style, but with less pronounced character. However, they have the same highly aromatic redcurranty nose and crisp fruit finish. The reds and rosés, made from the

Pinot Noir grape, are also very similar to their Sancerre counterparts, although a little less fine. Production is small, totalling 300,000 bottles of white wine and 130,000 bottles of red in an average year, the name little known, and the wines good value. Price C – D.

Pouilly-sur-Loire AOC

Dry white wine made from the Chasselas grape in the same region as Pouilly-Fumé. The Chasselas, which is also grown in Alsace and the Savoie, makes a light wine, 9° minimum, from the same yield as the Blanc-Fumé. It is a dry, fruity, light wine which is easy to drink, the perfect *vin de comptoir*. Production is only 300,000 bottles, and falling in favour of Pouilly-Fumé. There used to be a thriving sparkling wine industry in this region based on the Chasselas grape. None of the wine is exported, as it would lead to confusion with Pouilly-Fumé. Drink very young. Price D.

Quincy AOC

Dry white wines made exclusively from the Sauvignon in the communes of Quincy and Brinay in the Cher *département*. The wines of Quincy are very aromatic and of great finesse, and used to be sold under the *appellation* 'Quincy Vin Noble'. While its fruit is a little gooseberry-like and green in poor years, Quincy is usually softer, less assertive than Sancerre or Pouilly-Fumé, more distinctive than the neighbouring Ménétou-Salon and Reuilly. Can be kept, but should be drunk young for its charm. Minimum alcohol content 10.5°, yield 45 hl/ha. Price C – D.

Reuilly AOC

Dry white, red and rosé wines produced from the Sauvignon (whites), the Pinot Noir and Pinot Gris (reds and rosés) in vineyards planted on the banks of the Arnon, a tributary of the river Cher. The whites are typically 'Sauvignon du Centre de la Loire', fruity, aromatic and dry. They are comparable to Quincy in style, but more austere. The reds and rosés are lighter than the Sancerres, but have an interesting spiciness. Production is very small, averaging 100,000 bottles of white and 35,000 red and rosé, and the wines are drunk mostly in local restaurants where they show at their best. Price C – D.

Sancerre *AOC*

White, red and rosé wines grown around Sancerre and surrounding villages, on the left bank of the Loire, virtually opposite Pouilly-sur-Loire. The white Sancerre, representing over 80% of the production, must be made from the Sauvignon, with a minimum degree of 10.5° from a yield of 40 hl/ha. In plentiful years, such as 1982, this basic yield may be greatly increased. The style is much like Pouilly-Fumé, with perhaps a little more fruit and a little less elegance. But what differentiates one Sancerre from another, apart from the skill of the *propriétaire*, is the soil. There are three main types of soil in the *appellation*: the white, chalky soil on the steep slopes around Chavignol produces firm, elegant wines that may be kept; the stony soil on the lower slopes around Bué makes rounder, strikingly fruity wines which should be drunk young; the clayey soil on a chalky base from around Ménétréol produces wines which are less aggressively fruity than either Chavignol or Bué, but which have a soft elegance. White Sancerre is a most delicious wine which should be drunk relatively young, one to three years old, with hors d'œuvres, fish, white meats and the famous *crottin de Chavignol*. Red and rosé Sancerre are made from the Pinot Noir, which was the dominant grape in this region before the time of phylloxera, and is now only grown on soil unsuitable for the Sauvignon. The rosé is pale, salmon pink, and has the fruitiness of the Pinot Noir with the acidity of the Sauvignon. The red, which is only made in good years when sufficient colour can be obtained, is most interesting, a misplaced Burgundy with Loire Valley charm, well worth looking out for. Price D–E.

Châteaumeillant *VDQS*

Red and rosé wines from the south of the Cher *département*. The wines are made from the Gamay, Pinot Noir and Pinot Gris, with the Gamay dominant. Vines were already planted in this area in the twelfth century, and were very popular until phylloxera destroyed the vineyards. Less than 100 hectares are now planted. The red is very agreeable, light and fruity, with a pretty deep-cherry colour. It should be drunk quite young. The rosés are fruity and dry; especially good is the *vin gris* style of rosé, with very little colour but great delicacy of taste. Price C.

Coteaux du Giennois *VDQS*

Red, dry white and rosé wines made from grapes planted throughout the *départements* of Loiret and Nièvre, principally around Gien and Cosne-sur-Loire. These light, fruity, dry wines are made from the Sauvignon and Chenin Blanc for the whites and the Gamay and Pinot Noir for the red and rosé. They are light (9° minimum alcohol for reds and rosés, 10° for whites) and refreshing, and are perfect everyday table wines. Production is small and most of it is consumed locally. Price B–C.

Côte Roannaise *VDQS*

Red and rosé wines from the *département* of the Loire in the region of Renaison and Roanne. Wines are made from the Gamay, with a minimum alcohol content of 9° from a basic yield of 40 hl/ha. The style varies from a light, Beaujolais-type of wine to a deeper-coloured, more sturdy and more rustic wine from 'old-fashioned' *vignerons*. The latter can age well and tends to be more expensive. Production is small and very little is exported, since the wines are much sought after by the French themselves. Price C.

Côtes d'Auvergne *VDQS*

Red, dry white and rosé wines from the region of Clermont-Ferrand and Riom, in the *département* of Puy-de-Dôme. These are considered to be Loire wines, but they have little in common with the wines of Anjou and Touraine. The grape varieties for the red and rosé wines are the Gamay and a little Pinot Noir, which produce a wine of 9.5° minimum alcohol content from a basic yield of 45 hl/ha. The style is similar to Beaujolais, with an interesting *goût de terroir* of wild cherries, and sometimes a little more depth. They should be drunk young and served cool. Although 2 million bottles are produced annually, much of this is drunk locally, as the wine goes so well with the world-renowned *charcuterie d'Auvergne*. It also makes a pleasant change from the waters of the spa at Vichy. The better communes in the *appellation* have the right to add their name to that of Côtes d'Auvergne on the label, thus: Côtes d'Auvergne-Boudes, Côtes d'Auvergne-Chanturgue (historically the most famous), Côtes d'Auvergne-Corent, Côtes d'Auvergne-Madargues. The white wine, from the Chardonnay, is made in such small quantity as to be non-existent. The reds and rosés are perfect country wines. Price B–C.

Côtes du Forez *VDQS*

Red and rosé wines grown on the right bank of the upper stretches of the Loire, almost opposite Lyon. The only grape allowed is the Gamay, which makes light (9° minimum alcohol from a basic yield of 40 hl/ha), fruity wines, sometimes a little acidic in poor years, but generally very pleasing, Beaujolais in style; drink young. They are perfect with the local cuisine, where the wine's fruity acidity tempers the richness of the food, and are having a great success in Paris bistros. Very good value. Price B.

Saint-Pourçain-sur-Sioule *VDQS*

Red, dry white and rosé wines from the Allier *département*. These wines are considered as Loire wines, although by their *encépagement* they have more in common with Burgundy. The white wines must be from the local grape Tressalier (known as the Sacy in the region of Chablis), Chardonnay, Sauvignon, Aligoté and not more than 10% Saint-Pierre-Doré. They are light (9.5° minimum alcohol), with a transparent yellow-green colour, a fragrant, floral aroma and a deliciously refreshing, slightly appley taste. The red and rosé wines are made from the Pinot Noir and Gamay, and their style depends on the proportion of Pinot Noir. The lighter, Gamay-based wines closely resemble Beaujolais, those with more Pinot Noir are closer to Burgundy, while both have an attractive *goût de terroir*. The *vignerons* in Saint-Pourçain are determined to regain for their wines their historic reputation, and the wines represent excellent early drinking and value for money. Price B–C.

Vins de l'Orléanais *VDQS*

Red, white and rosé (especially *gris*) wines produced on both banks of the Loire in the region of Orléans. The white wines, under 10% of the production of 700,000 bottles, are made from the Pinot Blanc and Chardonnay. The reds and rosés are made from the Pinot Noir, Pinot Meunier and Cabernet. The red has a soft fruit (that belies its northern situation), owing to a short vinification, and should be drunk the year after the vintage. The best-known wine is the rosé from the Pinot Meunier, usually sold under the label Gris Meunier d'Orléans, very aromatic with a natural fruitiness. Most of the vineyards are owned by farmers more concerned with other crops, and very little leaves France. The wines are worth looking for in the bistros of Orléans, Chartres or Paris. Price B–C.

Vins de Pays

The Loire Valley, which would seem to be the obvious place to find a large number of local vins de pays, actually represents only 6% of the total production. Each *département* has its own vin de pays, but there are very few regional Vins de Pays de Zone. Perhaps one of the reasons is that the Loire Valley is one of the oldest vineyards in France, and its many local wines have become established earlier with their own *appellations*. As in the Rhône Valley, the vins de pays found in the Loire generally represent local grapes planted outside the accepted *appellation* or 'foreign' grapes planted within an already defined region. Price A.

Jardin de la France

The Vin de Pays du Jardin de la France is the largest of the three regional vins de pays, with a combined production of over 20 million bottles. Red, dry white and rosé wines are produced from the following *départements*: Cher, Indre, Indre-et-Loire, Loir-et-Cher, Loire-Atlantique, Loiret, Maine-et-Loire, Deux-Sèvres, Vendée, Vienne and the Haute-Vienne. This includes all the Val de Loire, and the varietals permitted are all those recommended in the Loire, as well as the Pinot Noir, Aligoté and Chardonnay from Burgundy. The wines, in general, are as delightful as their name: light, crisp whites, fruity, light-coloured reds and pretty, refreshing rosés. The style is typically 'Loire', and the wines are often as good as some of the lesser-known VDQS wines. They should all be drunk young and even the red wines are better drunk cool, especially the Gamay.

Thirteen *départements* across the Loire Valley have the right to their own vin de pays, the production in 1982 ranging from 5 million bottles in the Maine-et-Loire to under 9,000 in the Sarthe.

Cher

Red, dry white, *gris* and rosé wines made mostly from the Gamay and the Sauvignon, with a little Pinot Noir, Pinot Gris and Chardonnay. The Sauvignon whites resemble a Sancerre, and the Gamay reds a very light Beaujolais. All these wines have a refreshing acidity.

Deux-Sèvres

Red, dry white and rosé wines from the north of the *département*, most of the land being too rich to bear vines. They are light, low in alcohol and easy to drink.

Indre

Red, dry white, *gris* and rosé wines made from a large variety of Loire Valley grapes including the Cabernet Sauvignon. The rosés and light reds are the best, the whites tending to be a little tart. If the wine comes from a single grape varietal, it will state so on the label. The Gamay grape is most often used on its own.

Indre-et-Loire

Red, dry white and rosé wines from the heart of the Touraine vineyards. The excellent Sauvignon and Gamay wines from this *département* were all vins de pays until the better vineyards got the Touraine *appellation*. Sauvignon still plays a big part in the 3 million bottles sold but Chenin Blanc and Chardonnay are also used. These are some of the best vins de pays in the Loire Valley, the rosés are delightful, and the reds have more colour and flavour than one might expect.

Loir-et-Cher

Red, dry white, *gris* and rosé wines from the châteaux country around Blois, Chambord and Cheverny. Very big production of fruity but rather tart white wines from the Chenin Blanc and Sauvignon, light reds and rosés from the Gamay, Cot and Cabernet Franc. They resemble the wines of Cheverny and Coteaux du Vendômois, the two VDQS *appellations* in the *département*.

Loire-Atlantique

Red, dry white, *gris* and rosé wines that have much in common with the Vins de Pays des Marches de Bretagne et du Retz (see below) and the wines from the Coteaux d'Ancenis. Mostly white and very dry.

Loiret

Red, dry white, *gris* and rosé wines from the southern part of the *département* around Orléans and Gien. Gamay, Pinot Noir, Cabernet and Pinot Meunier are the grapes most used, with a little white made from the Sauvignon or the Chardonnay. The total production is limited and the wines are very light and do not travel.

Maine-et-Loire

Red, dry white and rosé wines from the Anjou country from the same grapes as the wines of Anjou (page 136) plus Gamay for the reds. The whites have a crisp, lemony flavour, and the reds and rosés are dry and fruity.

Nièvre

Red, dry white and rosé wines. Production is small and mostly white, fruity but with quite high acidity. Reds are made from the Gamay and Pinot Noir.

Puy de Dôme

Red, dry white and rosé wines from vines in the Côtes d'Auvergne region. Very small production of mostly red wines from the Gamay and the Pinot Noir.

Sarthe

Tiny production of mostly white wine from the Chenin Blanc, and a few reds and rosés from the Gamay, Cot and Cabernet Franc. The Sarthe is one of the few *départements* in France where the vine seems to be dying out.

Vendée

Very small production of wines similar to the local Vin de Pays des Fiefs Vendéens (see below).

Vienne

Red, dry white and rosé wines made from the same grape varieties as the Vins du Haut Poitou (page 142). Light and fruity wines. Small total production.

Vins de Pays de Zone

Coteaux du Cher et de l'Arnon

Red, dry white, *gris* and rosé wines from the *départements* of the Indre and the Cher. The better-known AOCs are Reuilly and Quincy. Reds and rosés are from the Gamay, with Pinot Noir and Pinot Gris; whites from the Sauvignon and Chardonnay, with Pinot Blanc up to 30%. These are delightful summer wines.

Fiefs Vendéens

Red, dry white and rosé wines from the Vendée *département*. Reds and rosés are from the Gamay, Cabernet Franc, Cabernet Sauvignon and Pineau d'Aunis; whites from the Gros Plant, Chenin Blanc, Sauvignon and Chardonnay, light and refreshing and should be drunk young. They are in the process of being accepted as VDQS.

Marches de Bretagne

Red, dry white and rosé wines from the south of the Loire-Atlantique *département*, the west of the Maine-et-Loire and the southern tip of the Vendée. Mostly whites, from the Muscadet, Folle Blanche, Sauvignon and Chenin, with a little Chardonnay; reds and rosés mostly from the Gamay and Cot. These are summer wines.

Retz

Red, dry white and rosé wines from the south-west of the Loire-Atlantique *département* and part of the Vendée. Mostly whites, from the Folle Blanche, Chenin Blanc and Sauvignon; reds and rosés made from the Gamay and Cot. Clean, pleasantly fresh wines.

Urfé

Red, dry white and rosé wines from the north of the Loire *département*. Reds and rosés from the Gamay and Pinot Noir; whites from the Chardonnay, Aligoté, Pinot Gris and Viognier. Not unlike Beaujolais in style.

Grape Varieties

The grape variety and the *terroir* (soil, sub-soil, climate) are the two vital elements that make up the profile, style or character of a wine. The human factor, which covers viticulture, vinification, *élevage* and bottling, is to a large extent determined by these two basic elements. In France, the interaction between grape variety and soil has been ratified in the Appellation Contrôlée system to set down ground rules for the production of some of the finest wines in the world. At the same time, varietals with distinctive character and quality (known as *cépages nobles*) have been replanted in 'foreign' soils in France and throughout the world to produce wines of intrinsic quality and recognizable style. It has been said that the character of a wine comes from the grape, its soul from the *terroir*.

Cépages Nobles (Red)

Cabernet Sauvignon
The principal grape of the Médoc and the basis of many of the finest wines in Bordeaux and the South-West, produces deep-coloured, intense wines that improve with age.

Cabernet Franc
A perfect foil to the Cabernet Sauvignon in the Bordeaux region, especially in the Graves, it is at its best in the Loire where it is known as le Breton and produces supple, elegant wines with a violet or raspberry aroma.

Merlot
Widely planted grape, most famous in Bordeaux, dominant in Saint-Emilion and Pomerol, blending with the Cabernets in the Médoc. Rich, full-bodied wines with a plummy, velvety fruit.

Pinot Noir
The traditional grape of Burgundy and north-eastern vineyards of France including Champagne and Alsace. Medium deep in colour, the wines have an elegant, strawberry-blackcurrant aroma and mature quite early.

Syrah
The principal grape for the great wines of the northern Rhône, also planted throughout the southern Rhône and Provence. Very deep-coloured wines, tannic with intense fruit, improving with age.

Mourvèdre
The principal grape for Bandol, and an important element in the wines of the Châteauneuf-du-Pape. Late-maturing, deep-coloured, austere wines, the perfect foil for Grenache.

Grenache
The most planted grape in the Rhône Valley producing fleshy, highly coloured wines. Also used to make VDNs in the Rhône and the Roussillon. When the yield exceeds 50 hl/ha, the wines lose character and definition.

Gamay
Producing violetty-red, fruity wines for early drinking. At its best in the Beaujolais and the Loire Valley. Does not do well in warm climates.

Cépages Nobles (White)

Chardonnay
The grape that produces all the great white Burgundies and the *blanc de blancs* Champagnes. The wines are pale golden in colour, rich in aroma, beautifully balanced and improve with age.

Chenin Blanc or Pineau de la Loire
Produces the finest wines in Touraine and Anjou in the full range from crisply dry to honey-sweet. Favourably susceptible to *pourriture noble*.

Sémillon
Planted principally in the Bordeaux region, where it is the basis for the great sweet wines, and throughout the South-West. As a dry wine it has a soft, subdued fruit and needs time to mature.

Sauvignon
Extremely versatile grape perhaps best known in the Loire Valley (Sancerre, Pouilly-Fumé) and beginning to rival the Sémillon in Bordeaux. An aggressively fruity wine with a marked blackcurrant/gooseberry bouquet and good acidity.

Riesling
The finest white grape variety along with Chardonnay. This and the other Alsatian varietals are referred to on pages 29–32.

Viognier
Rare grape planted exclusively in the northern Rhône Valley, producing the wines of Château Grillet and Condrieu. A wine of extraordinary finesse, aroma and richness, with a dry finish. May also be blended with the wines of Côte-Rotie.

Secondary Red Grapes

Carignan
The most planted grape in the Midi, producing dark-coloured, intense wines with a certain bitterness and lack of finesse.

Cinsault (Cinsaut)
Widely planted variety in the southern Rhône Valley, Provence and the Midi. Lightish in colour, with good fruit and acidity, wines from the Cinsault are an important foil to the Grenache for red wines, and essential for rosés.

Counoise
A Mediterranean varietal useful in Châteauneuf-du-Pape and wines from the Midi.

Cot or Malbec
Also known as the Auxerrois in Cahors, where it is dominant, and Pressac in Saint-Emilion. Generally used with other grapes for its colour and body, except in the Loire.

Fer or Fer-Servadou
Important indigenous grape in the South-West, making deep-coloured, slightly rustic wines with a firm backbone.

Gamay Teinturiers
The Gamay 'Beaujolais' has a colourless pulp, as do all red grapes for making fine wine. The juice of the Gamay Teinturiers is red, hence the name, used for adding colour to *vins ordinaires* and a few vins de pays.

Groslot or Grolleau
Red grape mostly planted in the Loire, where it is used principally for Anjou and Touraine rosés.

Mondeuse
Traditional grape of Savoy
and the Bugey, giving ruby-
coloured wines with good
body and flavour.

Niellucio
Grape variety indigenous to
Corsica, responsible for the
fine wines of Patrimonio.

Petit Verdot
One of the blender grapes
used in Bordeaux, hardly seen
now except in the Médoc.
Ripens fully only in good
years, giving the wine colour
and tannin.

Pineau d'Aunis
Grape planted in Touraine
and Anjou, used as a blender
grape for red wine, but more
often and more successfully on
its own for Loire rosés.

**Pinot Meunier or Gris
Meunier**
Grape of the Pinot family
making light red wines in the
Orléanais (Vin Gris
d'Orléans) and one of the
three grapes permitted in the
making of Champagne.

Poulsard
Varietal specific to the Jura,
where it gives a light-coloured
wine, more rosé than red.

Sciarello
Corsican varietal making fine,
deep-coloured wines with
body and fruit. Particularly
successful in the southern part
of the island.

Tannat
Grape variety particular to the
South-West, especially to the
wines of Madiran, dark in
colour, robust, tannic.

Trousseau
Varietal from the Jura, makes
a deep-coloured, long-lasting
wine, a complement to the
Poulsard and Pinot Noir.

Secondary White Grapes

Aligoté
Traditional Burgundy grape
making light dry wine, quite
high in acidity. At its best at
Bouzeron in the Saône-et-
Loire.

Altesse
Grape variety planted in
Savoy and the Bugey, making
firm, dry and very aromatic
white wines.

Auxerrois
A member of the Pinot family,
known in Alsace as Klevner,
producing firm, aromatic
wines without much finesse.

Bourboulenc
Southern grape variety seen in
the Côtes du Rhône
Méridionales throughout the
Midi and in the Minervois
where it is called Malvoisie,
producing fine aromatic wines
low in acidity that oxydise
quickly and should thus be
drunk young.

Chasselas
Better known as a table grape,
the Chasselas produces
pleasant, fruity wines for early
drinking in Alsace, the Savoy
and at Pouilly-sur-Loire.

Clairette
Traditional grape variety from
the Midi and the Côtes du
Rhône, producing a heady,
aromatic wine that should be
drunk young.

Colombard
Planted in the South-West,
the Colombard makes a
straightforward, fruity white
wine, as well as being one of
the principal grapes used to
produce Armagnac.

Folle Blanche
Grape used principally for distillation into Cognac and Armagnac, but capable of producing a pleasant white wine on its own, especially in the Loire-Atlantique where it is known as the Gros Plant du Pays Nantais.

Jacquère
One of the basic varietals for the *vins de Savoie*, light, slightly smokey bouquet, with a crisp fruit and pleasant acidity.

Maccabeo
Widely planted in the Languedoc-Roussillon, where it makes a full-bodied, aromatic, quite alcoholic white wine.

Marsanne
Now the major white grape variety in the northern Côtes du Rhône, also planted in the south. Fine, scented, full-bodied wines, the best of which is Hermitage.

Mauzac
Traditional grape variety of the South-West, around Gaillac and Limoux. Light and fresh, with an aromatic appley flavour, it is very good *champenisé*.

Muscadelle
One of the three grapes used to make the great sweet wine of Bordeaux and the South-West (with Sémillon and Sauvignon), normally used in small proportions owing to the very heady musky bouquet and rich sweet flavour.

Muscat à Petits Grains
The grape used to make the *vins doux naturels* at Frontignan, Rivesaltes, Beaumes-de-Venise etc.

Pinot Blanc
A grape of the Pinot family, still planted in Burgundy although it is inferior to the Chardonnay with which it has no connection. At its best in Alsace, where it produces aromatic, firm-flavoured wines that may be drunk young or kept.

Roussanne
Traditional grape from the northern Côtes du Rhône with more aroma and finesse than the Marsanne, with which it is being replaced.

Savagnin
Grape variety planted exclusively in the Jura where it makes very particular full-bodied wines with a distinctive sherry-like bouquet.

Ugni Blanc
Very widely planted grape in the south producing large quantities of straightforward wine, with an attractive flavour and acidity if the grapes are picked early. Also known as the Saint-Emilion in Charente, where it is distilled into Cognac.

Vermentino
Grape originally from Provence, but now mostly seen in Corsica under the name of Malvoisie, producing full-bodied, aromatic wines.

How and Where to Buy Country Wines

The availability of French country wines has improved so tremendously in the last five years that the range offered in London and New York is probably wider than in Paris, and shops throughout the United States and the United Kingdom will stock wines from all different parts of France, while provincial cities in France will tend to sell only wines from their region. On the other hand, the one great advantage of buying in France is that you can go directly to the producer. However, assuming that you are not in France and that the French wines you are buying are imported, you will for the most part be buying retail. The emergence, in the UK, of the supermarkets and mail-order companies selling a very well-chosen and competitively priced line of wines has forced the retailer to become more specialized and· to stock a more interesting range. In America, the dropping of resale price maintenance and the aggressive policies of large liquor stores has had the same effect. The consumer benefits greatly from this competition, particularly as the wines themselves are improving.

To make the most of the choice and the prices offered, comparative shopping and comparative tasting are equally important. It is better to try one bottle before buying a case of twelve, and if for reasons of transport you do have to buy a case, buy a mixed selection. Once you have found a wine you like and can drink on a variety of occasions at a price you can afford, then you can consider buying by the case. Do not stock up too much on light white wines or red wines to be drunk young. If the point of a wine is its freshness, buy no more than a few weeks' supply. If you do not have a cellar or anywhere dark where the temperature is not too variable, do not buy wines that are too young to drink. If they are stored in poor conditions, by the time they are at what should be their best, they will in fact be past it. One of the many charms of French country wines is that most of them are very good young.

What actual wines to buy is a matter of choice, but since price is affected by fashionability and supply, there are always some wines which are better value than others. The vintage plays some part, but as far as country wines are concerned, the most recent vintage is usually the one on offer, and this is often just as well. If in doubt, buy the latest vintage, but try to get some information first, either from your wine merchant or from a book. It pays to see which wines are in fashion, and therefore more highly priced, and to find out if there is a similar, but lesser, wine at a much lower price. Sancerre can be replaced by a Sauvignon de Touraine, for example, or Beaujolais by a Gamay du Lyonnais. Currently, good value in white wine is to be found in the Loire Valley, Bordeaux and Alsace, and for red wines in the southern Rhône, Bordeaux and the South-West. Vins de pays are very good value, but there are so many it is better to rely on the outlet where you buy than on the name of a producer. There are some very good sparkling wines made at Die, Gaillac and Limoux that make an inexpensive alternative to Champagne, and, with very few exceptions, *vins rosés* should never be expensive.

A very common complaint about country wines is that they do not travel. The ability of a wine to 'travel', to taste as good in the country where it is drunk as it does where it is made, is a function of two things: the alcoholic content and the image of the wine. Alcohol is the backbone of a wine, which supports the fruit, flavour and character. A wine light in alcohol, say under 10°, will not travel well, because it is too fragile. Most wines from the Bugey, for example, do not travel well, while robust wines of 11–13°, such as Corbières, travel splendidly. Then there is the image the wine projects, its *goût de terroir* particularly when associated with a meal or a place. Red wines from the Loire do not travel as well as red wines from Bordeaux. The reason in this case is that Bourgueil tastes better with the Loire cuisine in Touraine than with a steak in New York, while Bordeaux is more international. Furthermore, wines with high natural acidity taste mean and acid to palates accustomed to bland food and sweetened soft drinks. Finally, one cannot hope to reproduce the image of a wine, when there is an element missing. A chilled rosé de Provence will taste wonderful with a *salade niçoise* on the beach at Saint-Tropez, and perhaps less exciting in London. This is partly subjective, but mostly fact. The other fact is that local ambience will do wonders for a *vin ordinaire*, which is very *ordinaire* away from home ground.

In France, where the wines only have to travel as far as the next village, there is nothing better than to try the local vin de pays. If you want to buy some to take home, *vignerons* who sell direct put a sign up, and all Caves Coopératives sell as little as three bottles in take-away packs. If you have enjoyed a wine in a restaurant, the owner will be happy to telephone the supplier to make an appointment for you to go and taste. Because the prices will seem so inexpensive direct from the grower you should always buy the wine you like best, even if it costs a little more.

Wine and Food

Aperitifs	Shellfish	Fish	Charcuterie Foie gras	White meat Grilled poultry	Red meat	Red meat in sauce
●	●	●	●	●		
●		○	○	○		
●		○	●	●		
		○	●	●	●	●
			●	●	●	●
●	○	●	○	●		
●			○			

Order of Serving

1. White and rosé before red unless the white is a dessert wine. (Dry whites have a more marked acidity than reds, and this would be exaggerated coming at the end of a meal after a red.)

2. Dry white before sweet white; the same applies to rosés. (A sweet taste would smother the lighter flavour of a dry wine, as well as exaggerating its acidity.)

3. Light red before full-bodied red. (The more robust red would make the lighter wine taste insipid and thin.)

4. Young wines before old wines. (In general, young wines are not especially complex, while wines worth ageing gain in complexity. This rule may be broken if you want a refreshing glass of young red wine – Beaujolais, for example – after an old wine, but it is a risk.)

5. Dry sparkling wines at the beginning of a meal, sweeter sparkling wines at the end. (The acidity in a dry Champagne or sparkling wine is pleasant as an aperitif, or early in a meal, but unpleasantly tart with sweet desserts.)

6. Build up to quality, do not begin with it. (Keep the best wine until last, or for the high point of the meal. If it is served first, all following wines will be a disappointment.)

Game	Desserts	Cheese	Wines	Suggested wines
		○	Dry white	Vin de pays, Gros Plant, Alsace, Bordeaux (Graves, Entre-Deux-Mers), Saumur, Muscadet, Sancerre, Bourgogne, Côtes du Rhône, Savoie
	●		Sweet white	Sweet Bordeaux (Sauternes, Barsac), Coteaux du Layon, Vouvray, Alsace (Gewürztraminer), Monbazillac, Jurançon
○	○	○	Rosé	Vin de pays, Côtes de Provence, Touraine, Rosé de Loire, Côtes du Rhône (Lirac, Tavel), Rosé d'Anjou, Cabernet d'Anjou, Arbois, Béarn
●		●	Light red	Vin de pays (up to 11°), Bordeaux (Graves, Médoc), Beaujolais, Côtes de Beaune, Mâcon, Bergerac, Chinon, Bourgueil, Saumur Champigny, Corbières, Minervois, Costières du Gard, Coteaux du Languedoc, Gaillac
●		●	Full-bodied red	Vin de pays (over 11°), Côtes du Rhône, Bourgogne (Côtes de Nuits), Bordeaux (Saint-Emilion, Pomerol), Fitou, Côtes du Roussillon, Corsica, Cahors
	○	○	Sparkling and Champagne	Clairette de Die, Blanquette de Limoux, Crémant d'Alsace, Crémant de Bourgogne, Crémant de Loire, Gaillac, Champagne (all)
	●	○	Natural sweet wine	Maury, Rivesaltes, Rasteau, Banyuls, Muscat (various)

Temperature of Serving

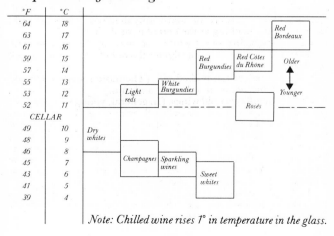

°F	°C	
64	18	
63	17	Red Bordeaux
61	16	
59	15	Red Burgundies, Red Côtes du Rhône
57	14	Older
55	13	White Burgundies
53	12	Light reds
52	11	Rosés — Younger
CELLAR		
49	10	Dry whites
48	9	
46	8	
45	7	Champagnes, Sparkling wines
43	6	
41	5	Sweet whites
39	4	

Note: Chilled wine rises 1° in temperature in the glass.

Vintage Chart

Scale of ratings

0–9	Bad, very poor, poor	14–15	Good
10–11	Acceptable	16–18	Very good
12–13	Quite good	19–20	Exceptional

		1970	71	72
Red Bordeaux	Médoc/Graves	19	17	11
	Saint-Emilion/Pomerol	19	18	10
White Bordeaux	Sauternes/Graves	17	17	11
Red Burgundy	Côte de Nuits	14	17	16
	Côte de Beaune	16	15	13
White Burgundy		16	16	12
Beaujolais		16	16	12
Rhône (North)	red	16	14	14
	white	16	15	10
Rhône (South)		14	16	15
Provence		15	15	11
Alsace		15	19	10
Loire	Muscadet/Anjou	14	15	10
	Touraine blanc	17	15	9
	Touraine rouge	17	15	9
	Sancerre/Pouilly-Fumé	14	19	8

Bottle Sizes and Shapes

A - Côtes du Rhône
B - Châteauneuf du Pape
C - Bordeaux Blanc
D - Bordeaux Rouge
E - Alsace
F - Bourgogne Blanc
G - Bourgogne Rouge
H - Occitane

A   B   C   D   E   F   G

73	74	75	76	77	78	79	80	81	82
13	13	18	15	13	19	17	14	17	19
13	13	18	16	12	18	18	13	16	19
13	12	18	16	12	14	16	14	17	16
13	13	5	18	10	19	15	16	13	14
13	12	7	18	11	19	16	13	13	13
16	13	13	16	12	18	17	12	17	16
16	12	13	17	8	19	15	12	16	14
13	14	9	16	13	20	16	15	13	15
14	15	8	17	14	17	18	17	17	18
13	13	10	16	12	19	15	16	14	12
12	15	18	11	14	18	15	16	17	16
16	13	16	19	12	15	14	13	17	15
13	10	14	16	10	16	15	13	14	15
13	11	14	17	10	16	14	12	17	14
13	12	13	19	10	15	14	11	13	15
16	14	16	18	12	17	15	15	16	14

I - Véronique
J - Hollandaise
K - Champenoise
L - Côtes de Provence (*négociant*)

M - Côtes de Provence
      (producer)
N - Corsica
O - Litre *6 étoiles*

H   I   J   K   L   M   N   O

Glossary

Appellation communale the *appellation* covering a commune, e.g. Pauillac, where there are different *crus* from specific vineyards.

Appellation contrôlée the system controlling what types of grapes may be planted where, what wine may be made from them and how, and what it will be called.

Botrytis cinerea noble rot or *pourriture noble* (q.v.).

Brut generally the driest version of Champagne and other sparkling wines. Wines totally without *dosage* (q.v.) are known as *brut zéro, brut de brut, brut intégral.*

Cépage noble one of the few grape varieties that consistently make fine wine.

Chambré used of a wine which has taken the temperature of the room after being brought from the cellar.

Champenisé used of wine that has been made sparkling by the *méthode champenoise* (q.v.).

Crémant sparkling wine that is less sparkling than Champagne or *vin mousseux* but more sparkling than a *vin pétillant.* The pressure inside the bottle is between 3 and 4 atmospheres.

Crus vineyards classified geographically or by reputation: *grand crus* (great growths), *premiers crus* (first growths) and so on.

Cuvée a wine from a selected barrel or vat, generally superior to the norm. In Champagne it means the wine from the first pressing.

Dégorgement the act of expulsion of sediment formed by the secondary fermentation in bottle to make a sparkling wine.

Demi-sec between sweet and dry, with the sweetness definitely discernible due either to residual sugar or to *dosage* (q.v.).

Dosage the sweetening of a sparkling wine, especially Champagne, to cover natural high acidity. According to the amount of sweetener added, the wine may be *brut, sec, demi-sec* or *doux* (qq.v.).

Doux fully sweet. The result of residual sugar in still wines, or *dosage* in sparkling wines.

Encépagement the make-up of grapes in a given wine.

En primeur used of a wine that is drunk very young.

En sec style of vinification to make dry wines of the wines that are traditionally sweet.

Garrigue tough, arid soil in the Southern Rhône Valley.

Générique a regional AOC wine without a *cru* or communal *appellation.*

Gouleyant used of a wine that is easy to drink.

Goût de terroir distinctive taste or style imparted by the combination of grape variety and soil.

Gravier gravelly soil, always found near a river. Tends to make elegant wines.

Gros rouge dull, heavy, uninteresting wine.

Liqueur d'expédition the sweetener used in the act of *dosage* (q.v.).

Liqueur de tirage the sugar added to a still wine at the time of bottling, to precipitate and prolong the secondary fermentation necessary to produce the required degree of sparkle.

Macération carbonique method of vinification in which the grapes are placed whole in the vats to achieve rapid fermentation under pressure from their natural gases. Used to produce fruity red wines for early drinking, typically in the Beaujolais and now in the Loire and Midi.

Méthode champenoise the method used in Champagne to make a still wine sparkle by means of secondary fermentation in bottle rather than in cask or vat. It is a long and expensive process, now used for most good sparkling wines.

Méthode dioise *see* Méthode rurale.

Méthode gaillaçoise *see* Méthode rurale.

Méthode rurale old-fashioned method of making sparkling wines, still used at Gaillac, Die and Limoux. No *liqueur de tirage* (q.v.) is added, the secondary fermentation taking place with sugar still present in the wine due to retarded alcoholic fermentation.

Moelleux very sweet, luscious white wines, between *doux* (q.v.) and *liquoreux.*

Négociant the middleman between the growers and the retailers.

Noble rot *see* Pourriture noble.

Perlé very slightly sparkling, often discernible only on the palate.

Pétillant semi-sparkling wine with not more than 3 atmospheres of pressure inside the bottle.

Pourriture noble noble rot, or the fungus which attacks white grapes in specific vineyards in the Loire Valley and the South-West, essential to making a great sweet white wine.

Sec dry, taken as meaning bone-dry except for sparkling wines, where it means a little less than dry.

Sur lie used of white wine which is bottled from the fine lees from the first (alcoholic) fermentation within the year following the vintage.

Teinturier grapes black grapes with coloured rather than colourless juice whose only positive role is to add colour to certain vins de pays.

Tendre delicate, soft, non-acidic wine, light and usually slightly sweet.

Terroir the combination of soil and climate. The main element in the taste of a wine along with the grape variety.

Tout court (e.g. Beaujolais) the simple *appellation*, as opposed to the Villages *appellation.*

Tris successive picking of a vineyard to harvest only the most ripe grapes.

Tuffeau chalky-clay soil in the Saumur and Touraine regions on which some of the best red wines are made.

Vendage tardive late picking of very ripe grapes.

Vin de base used in connection with sparkling wines to denote what the still wine was.

Vin de café red wine light in colour and alcohol.

Vin de carafe pleasant wine for everyday drinking.

Vin de comptoir generally pleasant wine for everyday drinking served in French cafés.

Vin-de-garde a wine which should be kept a long time.

Vin de pays everyday wine from a specific region, but less complexly controlled than AOC or VDQS wines.

Vin gris very pale rosé wine, almost grey in colour, always light and fresh.

Vin liquoreux very sweet white wine, generally made from grapes affected by *pourriture noble* (q.v.).

Vin mousseux sparkling wine, made either by secondary fermentation in bottle or in tank, or, for inexpensive wines, by the addition of carbon dioxide.

Vin ordinaire plain wine with no regional or varietal origin.

Vin tranquille non-sparkling wine.

Comités Interprofessionels Vins et Spiritueux

These semi-public bodies, which are made up both of delegates of the producers and the *négociants*, and of representatives of the various administrative services, play an important role at all levels of wine production and marketing. One of their functions is to inform the consumer: most of them have a secretariat and a variety of informational material, such as maps and brochures. Anyone who requires information about a specific wine-producing area should apply to the organization responsible for that particular region.

Alsace

C.I.V.A., Comité interprofessionnel des vins d'Alsace, 8, place de-Lattre-de-Tassigny, 68003 Colmar Cedex.

Beaujolais

U.I.V.B., Union interprofessionnelle des vins du Beaujolais, 210, boulevard Vermorel, 69400 Villefranche-sur-Saône.

Burgundy/Mâcon

C.I.B.M., Comité interprofessionnel des vins de Bourgogne et Mâcon, Maison du tourisme, avenue du Maréchal-de-Lattre-de-Tassigny, 71000 Mâcon.

Côte-d'Or/Yonne

C.I.B., Comité interprofessionnel de la Côte-d'Or et de l'Yonne pour les vins A.O.C. de Bourgogne, rue Henri-Dunant, 21200 Beaune.

Bordeaux

C.I.V.B., Conseil interprofessionnel du vin de Bordeaux, 1, cours du 30 juillet, 33000 Bordeaux.

Bergerac

C.I.V.R.B., Comité interprofessionnel des vins de la région de Bergerac, 2, place du docteur-Cayla, 24100 Bergerac.

Champagne

C.I.V.C., Comité interprofessionnel du vin de Champagne, B.P. 135, 51204 Épernay Cedex.

Côtes de Provence

C.I.V.C.P., Comité interprofessionnel des vins des Côtes de Provence, 3, avenue Jean-Jaurès, 83460 Les-Arcs-sur-Argens.

Côtes du Rhône

C.I.C.D.R., Comité interprofessionnel des vins des Côtes du Rhône, Maison du tourisme et du vin, 41, cours Jean-Jaurès, 84000 Avignon.

Fitou/Corbières/Minervois

Conseil interprofessionnel des vins de Fitou, Corbières et Minervois, R.N. 113, 11200 Lézignan-Corbières.

Gaillac

C.I.V.G., Comité interprofessionnel des vins de Gaillac, 8, rue du Père Gibrat, 81600 Gaillac.

Anjou/Saumur

C.I.V.A.S., Conseil interprofessionnel des vins d'Anjou et de Saumur, 21, boulevard Foch, 49000 Angers.

Pays Nantais

C.I.V.O.P.N., Comité interprofessionnel des vins d'origine du Pays Nantais, 17, rue des États, 44000 Nantes.

Vins Doux Naturels

C.I.V.D.N., Comité interprofessionnel des vins doux naturels, 19, avenue de Grande-Bretagne, 66000 Perpignan.

Touraine

C.I.V.T., Comité interprofessionnel des vins de Touraine, 19, square Prosper-Mérimée, 37000 Tours.

Corsica

Groupement interprofessionnel des vins de l'Ile de Corse, 6, rue Gabriel-Péri, 20000 Bastia.

Bibliography

Blanchet, Suzanne, *Les Vins du Val de Loire*, ed. Jema SA, Saumur, 1982.

Brejoux, Pierre, *Les Vins de la Loire*, ed. Revue de Vin de France.

Brunel, Gaston, *Guide des Vignobles et Caves des Côtes du Rhône*, ed. L.-C. Lattes, Paris, 1980.

Debuigne, G., *Dictionnaire des Vins*, ed. Larousse.

Duijker, Hubert, *The Loire, Alsace and Champagne*, Mitchell Beazley, 1982.

Dumay, Raymond, *Guide du Vin*, ed. Stock.

Hanson, Anthony, *Burgundy*, Faber, London, 1982; Boston, 1983.

Johnson, Hugh, *The World Atlas of Wine*, Mitchell Beazley, London, 1977; Simon and Schuster, 1978.

Lichine, Alexis, *Encyclopedia of Wines and Spirits*, Alfred A. Knopf, New York, 1974; Cassell, London, 1978.

Livingstone-Learmonth, John and Master, Melvyn, *The Wines of the Rhône*, Faber, London, 1983; Boston, 1983.

Poulain, René and Jacquelin, Louis, *Vignes et Vins de France*, ed. Flammarion.

Ray, Cyril, *The Wines of France*, Allen Lane, 1976.

Woutaz, Fernand, *Dictionnaire des Appellations*, ed. Litec, Paris, 1982.

Index

A

Agenais, 130
Alsace, 29–33
Alsace AOC, 29
Alsace Grand Cru AOC, 32
Anjou AOC, 136
Anjou Coteaux de la Loire AOC, 137
Anjou Gamay AOC, 137
Anjou Mousseux AOC, 137
Arbois AOC, 23
Arbois Mousseux AOC, 23
Arbois Pupillin AOC, 23
Ardaillon, 86
Argens, 76
Aude Département, 89–94
Auxerrois *see* Klevner
Auxey-Duresses AOC, 42
Ayse *see* Vin de Savoie

B

Balmes Dauphinoises, 28
Bandol AOC, 72
Banyuls VDN, 101
Banyuls Grand Cru VDN, 101
Banyuls Rancio VDN, 101
Barsac, 104, 106
Béarn AOC, 119
Beaujolais AOC, 50–1
Beaujolais Bâtard AOC, 50
Beaujolais Crus, 51–3
Beaujolais Supérieur AOC, 50–1
Beaujolais-Villages AOC, 51
Beaumes-de-Venise VDN, 54, 62
Bellegarde, Clairette de, 78
Bellet, 72
Bénovie, 86
Bérange, 86
Bergerac AOC, 119, 125
Bergerac sec AOC, 120
Bessans, 86
Blanc Fumé de Pouilly AOC, 150
Blanquette de Limoux AOC, 89
Blaye or Blayais, 111–12
Bonnezeaux AOC, 137
Bordeaux, 102–18
Bordeaux AOC, 104
Bordeaux Clairet AOC, 104
Bordeaux Mousseux AOC, 105
Bordeaux Rosé AOC, 105
Bordeaux Supérieur AOC, 105
Bordeaux Supérieur-Côtes de Castillon AOC, 105
Bordeaux Supérieur-Côtes de Francs AOC, 106
Bordeaux Supérieur – Haut-Bénauge AOC, 106
Bourg-Bourgeais AOC, 112
Bourgueil AOC, 143
Bourgogne AOC, 36–7
Bourgogne Aligoté AOC, 37, 44, 47
Bourgogne Aligoté de Bouzeron AOC, 45
Bourgogne Clairet AOC, 37
Bourgogne Grand Ordinaire AOC, 37, 44, 47

Bourgogne Hautes-Côtes-de-Beaune AOC, 43
Bourgogne Hautes-Côtes-de-Nuits AOC, 40–1
Bourgogne Irancy AOC, 39
Bourgogne Passe-Tout-Grains AOC, 38, 44, 47, 48
Bourgogne Rosé AOC, 37, 38
Bourgogne Rosé de Marsannay AOC, 41
Bourgogne Rouge de Marsannay AOC, 41
Brouilly AOC, 51
Bugey *see* Vin du Bugey
Burgundy, 34–53

C

Cabardès VDQS, 89–90
Cabernet d'Anjou AOC, 138
Cabernet d'Anjou-Val-de-Loire AOC, 138
Cabernet de Saumur AOC, 138
Cabrières VDQS, 82
Cadillac AOC, 107
Cahors AOC, 120
Cairanne AOC, 63
Canon Fronsac AOC, 113
Cassan, 88
Cassis AOC, 72
Catalan, 97
Caux, 86
Cérons AOC, 107
Cessenon, 86
Chablis AOC, 34, 39–40
Charentais, 130
Chasselas (grape), 29
see also Grape varieties
Château-Chalon, 24
Châteaumeillant VDQS, 152
Châteauneuf-du-Pape AOC, 61
Châtillon-en-Diois AOC, 59
Cheilly-lès-Maranges AOC, 43
Chénas AOC, 52
Cher, 155
Cheverny VDQS, 148–9
Cheverny-Gamay, 149
Chignin, 27
Chinon AOC, 143
Chiroubles AOC, 52
Chorey-lès-Beaune AOC, 43
Chusclan AOC, 63
Clairet de Marsannay, 41
Clairette de Bellegarde AOC, 78
Clairette de Die AOC, 59
Clairette du Languedoc AOC, 81
Clairette du Languedoc Rancio AOC, 81
Collines de la Moure, 86
Collines Rhodaniennes, 68
Collioure AOC, 95
Comté de Grignan, 69
Comté Tolosan, 130
Condomois, 130
Condrieu, 54
Corbières VDQS, 90
Corbières Supérieures VDQS, 90
Corsican wines, 97–100

Cornas AOC, 57
Costières du Gard VDQS, 78
Côte Chalonnaise, 44–6
Côte de Beaune AOC, 34, 42–4
Côte de Beaune-Villages AOC, 43, 44
Côte-de-Brouilly AOC, 52
Côte de Nuits AOC, 34, 40–2
Côte de Nuits-Villages AOC, 41, 42
Côte d'Or, 34, 40–44
Côte Roannaise VDQS, 153
Côte-Rôtie, 57
Coteaux Cathares, 92
Coteaux Cévenols, 79
Coteaux d'Aix-en-Provence VDQS, 74
Coteaux d'Ancenis VDQS, 135
Coteaux de Baronnies, 69
Coteaux de Cèze, 79
Coteaux de Fontcaude, 86
Coteaux de Glanes, 130
Coteaux de la Cabrerisse, 92
Coteaux de la Cité de Carcassonne, 92
Coteaux de la Méjanelle VDQS, 82
Coteaux de l'Ardèche, 69
Coteaux de l'Aubance AOC, 138
Coteaux de Laurens, 87
Coteaux de Lézignanais, 92
Coteaux de Libron, 87
Coteaux de Miramont, 92
Coteaux de Murviel, 87
Coteaux de Narbonne, 93
Coteaux de Peyriac, 87, 93
Coteaux de Pierrevert VDQS, 75
Coteaux de Quercy, 131
Coteaux de Saint-Christol VDQS, 82
Coteaux de Saumur AOC, 138, 140
Coteaux de Termenès, 93
Coteaux de Vérargues VDQS, 82
Coteaux d'Enserune, 86
Coteaux des Baux-en-Provence VDQS, 75
Coteaux des Fenouillèdes, 97
Coteaux du Cher et de l'Arnon, 157
Coteaux du Giennois VDQS, 153
Coteaux du Gréstvaudan, 29
Coteaux du Languedoc VDQS, 82–3
Coteaux du Layon AOC, 137, 139
Coteaux du Layon-Chaume AOC, 139
Coteaux du Littoral Audois, 93
Coteaux du Loir, 144
Coteaux du Lyonnais VDQS, 53
Coteaux du Pont-du-Gard, 79
Coteaux du Salagou, 87
Coteaux du Tricastin AOC, 60
Coteaux du Vendômois VDQS, 149
Coteaux du Vidourle, 80
Coteaux et Terrasses de Montauban, 131
Coteaux Flaviens, 80

Coteaux Varois, 76
Côtes Catalanes, 97
Côtes d'Agly VDN, 101
Côtes d'Auvergne, VDQS, 153
Côtes de Bergerac AOC, 120
Côtes de Bergerac – Côtes de Saussignac AOC, 121
Côtes de Bergerac Moelleux AOC, 121
Côtes de Blaye AOC, 112
Côtes de Bordeaux Saint-Macaire AOC, 107
Côtes de Bourg AOC, 112
Côtes de Brian, 87
Côtes de Buzet AOC, 121
Côtes de Castillon AOC (Bordeaux Supérieur), 105
Côtes de Céressou, 87
Côtes de Duras AOC, 122
Côtes de Francs AOC (Bordeaux Supérieur), 106
Côtes de Fronsac *see* Fronsac
Côtes de Gascogne, 131
Côtes de la Malepère VDQS, 90–1
Côtes de Lastours, 93
Côtes de Montestruc, 131
Côtes de Montravel AOC, 122
Côtes de Pérignan, 93
Côtes de Provence AOC, 73
Côtes de Prouille, 93
Côtes de Saint-Mont VDQS, 128
Côtes de Saussignac AOC, 121
Côtes de Thau, 87
Côtes de Thongue, 87
Côtes de Toul VDQS, 33
Côtes du Bruhlois, 131
Côtes du Cabardès et de l'Orbiel, 89
Côtes du Forez VDQS, 154
Côtes du Frontonnais AOC, 122
Côtes du Jura AOC, 23–4
Côtes du Jura Mousseux AOC, 24
Côtes du Luberon VDQS, 67
Côtes du Marmandais VDQS, 128
Côtes du Rhône, 54–69
Côtes du Rhône AOC, 56
Côtes du Rhône-Villages AOC, 56, 61, 62
Côtes du Roussillon AOC, 95
Côtes du Roussillon-Villages AOC, 96
Côtes du Salavès, 80
Côtes du Tarn, 131
Côtes du Ventoux AOC, 66
Côtes du Vivarais VDQS, 60
Crémant d'Alsace AOC, 31, 33
Crémant de Bourgogne AOC, 38, 44, 47
Crémant de Loire AOC, 139
Crépy AOC, 25, 29
Crozes-Hermitage AOC, 57–8
Cucugnan, 93
Cuvée Napoléon, 121

D
Deux-Sèvres, 155
Dezize-lès-Maragues AOC, 43
Die, Clairette de, 59

E
Edelzwicker, 29, 30
Entre-Deux-Mers AOC, 108
L'Etoile, 24
L'Etoile Mousseux, 24

F
Faugères AOC, 81
Fiefs Vendéens, 157
Fitou AOC, 89
Fixin AOC, 40, 42
Fleurie AOC, 52
Folle-Blanche *see* Gros Plant du
    Pays Nantais
Franche-Comté, 29
Frangy, 25
Fronsac AOC, 113

G
Gaillac AOC, 122–3
Gaillac doux AOC, 123
Gaillac Mousseux AOC, 123
Gaillac Perlé AOC, 124
Gaillac Premières Côtes AOC,
    124
Gard Département, 78–80
Gewürztraminer, 30, 32
Gigondas AOC, 66
Givry AOC, 45
Gorges de l'Hérault, 88
Gorges et Côtes de Millau, 131
Grand Roussillon VDN, 101
Grave AOC, 108–9
Graves Supérieures AOC, 109
Graves de Vayres AOC, 109
Gris Meunier (Vins de
    l'Orléanais), 154
Gros Plant du Pays Nantais
    VDQS, 135

H
Haut-Bénauge AOC (Bordeaux
    Supérieur), 106
Haut-Comtat VDQS, 60
Haut-Médoc AOC, 116, 117–18
Haut Montravel AOC, 122
Haute Vallée de l'Aude, 93–4
Haute Vallée de l'Orb, 85, 88
Hautrive en Pays de l'Aude, 94
Hauts de Badens, 94
Hérault Département, 81–8
Hermitage, 54, 57

I
Ile de Beauté, 100
Indre, 155
Indre-et-Loire, 156
Irouléguy AOC, 124

J
Jardin de la France *see* Vin de Pays
Jasnières AOC, 144
Juliénas AOC, 52
Jura, 23–4
Jurançon AOC, 124–5
Jurançon sec AOC, 125

K
Klevner or Clevner, 30

L
La Clape VDQS, 83
Lalande de Pomerol AOC, 113,
    114
Languedoc, Clairette du, 81
Laudun AOC, 63
Lirac AOC, 66–7, 79
Listel (Les Salins du Midi), 77
Listrac AOC, 117
Littoral Orb-Hérault, 88
Loire-Atlantique, 156
Loire Valley, 132–57
Loiret, 156
Loir-et-Cher, 156
Lorraine, 33
Loupiac AOC, 109
Lussac Saint-Emilion AOC, 114

M
Mâcon (Blanc) AOC, 47
Mâcon (Blanc) Supérieur AOC,
    47
Mâcon (Rouge or Rosé) AOC, 47
Mâcon Supérieur (Rouge or
    Rosé) AOC, 48
Mâcon-Villages or Mâcon +
    commune AOC, 48
Mâconnais, 46–9
Madiran AOC, 125
Maine-et-Loire, 156
Marches de Bretagne, 157
Margaux AOC, 117
Marignan, 27
Marsannay, Bourgogne Rosé et
    Rouge de, 41
Maures, 76
Maury VDN, 101
Médoc AOC, 116–18
Ménétou-Salon AOC, 150–1
Mercurey AOC, 45
Minervois VDQS, 91
Monbazillac AOC, 126
Mont Baudile, 88
Mont Bouquet, 80
Mont Caume, 77
Montpeyroux VDQS, 83
Montagne Saint-Emilion AOC,
    114
Montagny AOC, 46
Monterminod, 25
Montlouis AOC, 144
Montlouis Mousseux AOC, 145
Montlouis Pétillant AOC, 145
Monthoux, 25
Montravel AOC, 122, 126
Monts de la Grage, 88
Morgon AOC, 53
Moulin-à-Vent AOC, 53
Moulis AOC, 117
Muscadet AOC, 134
Muscadet des Coteaux de la Loire
    AOC, 134
Muscadet de Sèvre-et-Maine
    AOC, 135
Muscat d'Alsace, 30, 32
Muscat-de-Beaumes de Venise,
    54, 62
Muscat de Frontignan VDN, 101

Muscat de Lunel AOC, 86, 101
Muscat de Miréval VDN, 101
Muscat de Rivesaltes VDN, 101
Muscat de Saint-Jean-de-
  Minervois VDN, 101

N
Néac AOC, 114
Nièvre, 156

P
Pacherenc du Vic Bihl AOC, 127
Palette AOC, 72, 74
Parsac-Saint-Emilion AOC, 114
Pauillac AOC, 118
Pécharmant AOC, 127
Petit Chablis AOC, 40
Petite Crau, 77
Pézenas, 88
Picpoul de Pinet VDQS, 83
Pic-Saint-Loup VDQS, 84
Pinot Blanc, 30, 31
  see also Grape varieties
Pinot-Chardonnay-Mâcon AOC,
  47
Pinot Gris (Tokay d'Alsace), 32
Pinot Noir, 31
  see also Grape varieties
Pomerol AOC, 114
Pouilly-Fuissé AOC, 49
Pouilly-Fumé (Blanc Fumé), 150
Pouilly-Loché AOC, 49
Pouilly-sur-Loire AOC, 151
Pouilly-Vinzelles AOC, 49
Premières Côtes de Blaye AOC,
  112
Premières Côtes de Bordeaux
  AOC, 110
Premières Côtes de Bordeaux-
  Cadillac AOC, 107
Principauté d'Orange, 69
Puisseguin-Saint-Emilion AOC,
  115
Puy de Dôme, 156
Pyrénées-Orientales
  Département, 95–7

Q
Quarts de Chaume AOC, 139
Quatourze VDQS, 84
Quincy AOC, 151

R
Rappu VDN, 99
Rasteau AOC, 63
Rasteau VDN, 63
Retz, 157
Reuilly AOC, 151
Rhône Valley, 54–69
Riesling, 31, 32
Ripaille, 27
Rivesaltes VDN, 101
Roaix AOC, 64
Rochegude AOC, 64
Rosé d'Anjou, 140
Rosé d'Anjou Pétillant AOC, 140
Rosé de Loire AOC, 140
Rosette AOC, 127
Rousset AOC, 60, 64

Roussette de Savoie AOC, 25
Roussette de Savoie + Cru
  AOC, 25
Rully AOC, 46

S
Sables du Golfe du Lion, 77, 80,
  88
Sablet AOC, 64
Saint-Amour, 53
Saint-Aubin AOC, 44
Saint-Chinian AOC, 81
Saint-Drézery VDQS, 84
Saint-Emilion AOC, 115
Saint-Estèphe AOC, 118
Saint-Georges d'Orques VDQS,
  84
Saint-Georges-Saint-Emilion
  AOC, 116
Saint-Gervais AOC, 64
Saint-Joseph AOC, 58
Saint-Julien AOC, 118
Saint-Maurice-sur-Eygues AOC,
  64
Saint-Nicolas-de-Bourgueil
  AOC, 145
Saint-Pantaléon-les-Vignes, 60, 64
Saint-Péray AOC, 58
Saint-Péray Mousseux AOC, 58
Saint-Pourçain-sur-Sioule
  VDQS, 154
Saint-Romain AOC, 44
Saint-Sardon, 131
Saint-Saturnin VDQS, 84
Saint-Véran AOC, 49
Sainte-Croix-du-Mont AOC, 110
Sainte-Foy-Bordeaux AOC,
  110–11
Les Salins du Midi (Listel), 77
Sampigny-lès-Maragnes AOC, 43
Sancerre AOC, 152
Sarthe, 157
Satellite-Saint-Emilions, 114, 116
Saumur AOC, 140
Saumur-Champigny AOC, 140–1
Saumur Mousseux AOC, 141
Saumur Pétillant AOC, 141
Sauternes AOC, 104, 111
Sauvignon de Saint-Bris VDQS,
  40
Savennières AOC, 141
Savennières-Coulée-de-Serrant
  AOC, 142
Savennières-Roche-aux-Moines
  AOC, 142
Savoie, 25–7
Séguret AOC, 65
Serre de Coiran, 80
Seyssel AOC, 26
Seyssel Mousseux AOC, 26
SICAREX, 77
South-West France, 119–31
Sylvaner d'Alsace, 31–2

T
Tavel AOC, 67, 79
Tokay d'Alsace or Pinot Gris, 32
Touraine, 142–9
Touraine AOC, 145–6

Touraine-Amboise AOC, 146
Touraine-Azay-le-Rideau AOC, 146
Touraine-Mesland AOC, 146–7
Touraine Mousseux AOC, 147
Touraine Pétillant AOC, 147
Tricastin *see* Coteaux du Tricastin
Tursan VDQS, 128

U
Urfé, 157
Uzège, 80

V
Vacqueyras AOC, 65
Val de Cesse, 94
Val d'Agly, 97
Val de Dagne, 94
Val de Montferrand, 88
Val d'Orbieu, 94
Valençay VDQS, 149
Vallée de Paradis, 94
Valréas AOC, 65
Vaunage, 80
Vendée, 157
Vicomté d'Aumelas, 88
Vienne, 157
Vin de Corse AOC, 98
Vin de Corse Sartène AOC, 100
Vin de Corse Calvi AOC, 98
Vin de Corse Coteaux d'Ajaccio AOC, 99
Vin de Corse Coteaux du Cap Corse AOC, 99
Vin de Corse Figari AOC, 99
Vin de Corse Patrimonio AOC, 99
Vin de Corse de Porto-Vecchio AOC, 100
Vin de paille, 20, 24
Vin de Pays de la Dordogne, 130
Vin de Pays de la Drôme, 68
Vin de Pays de la Gironde, 130
Vin de Pays de la Meuse, 33
Vin de Pays de l'Ain, 29
Vin de Pays de l'Ardèche, 68
Vin de Pays de l'Aude, 91–4
Vin de Pays de l'Hérault, 85–8

Vin de Pays de l'Yonne, 53
Vin de Pays des Alpes-de-Haute-Provence, 75
Vin de Pays des Alpes-Maritimes, 75
Vin de Pays des Bouches-du-Rhône, 76
Vin de Pays des Collines de la Moure, 85, 86
Vin de Pays des Landes, 130
Vin de Pays des Pyrénées-Orientales, 96–7
Vin de Pays d'Oc, 96
Vin de Pays du Gard, 79–80
Vin de Pays du Jardin de la France, 155–7
Vin de Pays du Var, 76
Vin de Pays du Vaucluse, 68
Vin de Savoie AOC, 26
Vin de Savoie + Cru AOC, 26–7
Vin de Savoie Ayse Mousseux AOC, 27
Vin de Savoie Mousseux AOC, 27
Vin du Bugey VDQS, 27–8
Vin du Bugey + Cru VDQS, 28
Vin du Bugey Mousseux or Pétillant VDQS, 28
Vin fou, 23
Vin gris, 33
Vin jaune, 20, 24
Vin Noble du Minervois VDQS, 91
Vins de Lavilledieu VDQS, 129
Vins de l'Orléanais VDQS, 154
Vins de Marcillac VDQS, 129
Vins de Moselle VDQS, 33
Vins d'Entraygues et du Fel VDQS, 129
Vins d'Estaing VDQS, 129
Vins doux naturels (VDN), 101
Vins du Haut Poitou VDQS, 142
Vins du Thouarsais VDQS, 142
Vinsobres AOC, 65
Visan AOC, 65
Vistrenque, 80
Vouvray AOC, 147–8
Vouvray Mousseux AOC, 148
Vouvray Pétillant AOC, 148

Acknowledgements

For such a large and changing subject as French country wines, research in the form of reading, travelling and tasting could take a lifetime. However, as this is basically a guide-book, and not an attempt at a definitive work, it has been written with experience acquired from many years in France, buying, selling and drinking these wines. For reference I have relied on the *Dictionnaire des Vins* by G. Debuigne and the *Dictionnaire des Appellations* by Fernand Woutaz. M. le Pechou at SOPEXA and M. Davesne at ONIVIT provided me with much-needed figures and facts, but, as M. Davesne told me, there is no official information on vins de pays, and I should have waited until *his* book comes out next year. Much of the last-minute research was done by Isabelle Bachelard of L'Académie du Vin, at a time when she had better things to do, and while some of the wine labels were provided by the growers, or Comités Interprofessionels, the majority were soaked off the bottles in the Caves de la Madeleine by the indomitable Mamicette Thovan.

Special thanks are due to Yapp of Mere (Wiltshire) and Michael Druitt Wines of London for wine labels.

Maps © SOPEXA (p. 19 SOPEXA original; pp. 20–1, 35, 55, 71, 103, 133 redrawn by kind permission).

Temperature chart (p. 165) reproduced by permission of M. Dovaz and Editions Vecchi.

Illustrations p. 166 by TIGA.

Jacket illustration Mary Evans Picture Library.